Let's Get Shift Done.

Manifesting Your Destiny with a Sound Mind

Find your focus, acquire motivation, and develop the tools you need to embrace a radical *shift* in your life!

Millie 'Joy' Radosti

This book contains material that might not be suitable for all readers. Some of the content of this book is of a graphic nature and is intended for mature audiences only. Please use discretion when reading this book.

Table of Contents

⬆SHIFT Introduction

I'm so glad you picked up this book. Why? Because if you've read up to this sentence, I know a bit about the person you are. You've had dreams in your life that might be buried under some fear. They might not be buried miles deep but just under a couple layers of "life got in the way," or "I was scared to fail." Maybe they're buried under some layers of "I was in season after season of putting others before myself." Or maybe they're even buried under miles of guilt, fear, condemnation, and shame due to some unfortunate life paths you've been journeying. Some of you reading this are already on the road to seeing your dreams manifest, but you're taken a lot of rabbit trails from what you originally expected. Maybe you've seen a lot of success, but you don't want to burn out and even thought you'd have progressed further by now. This book is for you! I want to take

1

the dreams and passions buried under all those layers and see you manifest victoriously and successfully while thriving in your personal life. You will find the keys in these pages to motivation and focus while developing your character and improving your overall quality of life. I know you will benefit from not only gaining this practical knowledge but from seeing the fruit of practicing it in your lifestyle. Take notes, and read this book again and again. Don't settle until you have reached the full potential you are satisfied with! Enjoy!

I was a fitness coach for many years, and though I absolutely loved the company and what they stand for, I found that, to my surprise, people continually came to me and wanted to know how to motivate themselves and not necessarily how to lose weight. They had tried everything available to reach their goals but nothing worked. I was in a business seminar once for a different company that said "this business works for anyone if they work the business!" That's just the thing— people will try a million things, but never follow through with one! You see, in the beginning, when you're about to embark on an adventure, all your steam, focus, and motivation is driven by the freshness of the vision. In laymen's terms, you are running off hype. When someone wants to start a new fitness goal, they will often do much better on the first day than on any other day after that. Why is that? Your body pumps all these adrenaline hormones through you that says, "You thought couldn't do it! But now, you're doing it! And look, it's pain free!"

But what happens the next day is very unsettling. The soreness and pain set in, and not only is it difficult to run, but it's difficult to even *move*! You can hardly climb the stairs or use the bathroom without excruciating pain.

But still yet, you push through. Why? Because the biggest killer of motivation is— get this—*not* pain and not even challenge! The biggest motivation killer is boredom. Mundane, passionless, dutiful, daunting routines that make you wonder why you are doing what you are doing in the first place. People feel like a champ if they make it through their first week of exercise on a new plan. I say they are a champ if they make it to week eight!

So how do we stay motivated when we have no more pain to conquer and no more hype to motivate us? This is the focus of my book. I want to dig into the core of who you are to again spark those passions that led you to your daydreams so that you can, in turn, make your daydreams a reality!

When reading through this book, you will naturally reflect on areas of your own life that apply to you. Don't ignore those thoughts but let them surface, even if you put the book down for a minute. Let the principle you were learning about what ignited that thought take its full course. See if and how you can incorporate these practices in your current situation. *Envision* improvement! Let your mind and heart take you to the mountaintops of victory in your life. For every great action is first a thought with a plan of execution. Together we will draw a personal road map to success. It *must* be personal because no two roads will look exactly the same. And no road is traveled exactly as it is paved either. So we will make room for improvement on our journey, for mistakes that lead to growth, and for disappointments that lead to knowledge. No discouragement is too great to overcome except the acceptance of failure as permanent.

My first challenge to you, the reader, before I even close out this introduction, is to make a promise to yourself that you will not give up. In fact, this is less of a promise and more of a covenant. I say this because a promise is a definite assurance while a covenant is more of an agreement you have with yourself. An agreement can be modified to fit the overall direction of your success and that flexibility will be key in propelling you toward your destiny. Be flexible with yourself but also be very clear in your mission. Decide today that you will do what you've set your heart to do. Make it your confession and do not waver from it.

"Let us hold fast the confession of our hope without wavering, for he who promised is faithful" (Hebrews 10:23 ESV).

Starting today, we will build your road map together. Hang on tight and get excited. *Let's get shift done!*

Chapter 0

The Chapter before Chapter 1: The Most Foundational Concept

Everyone has a personal value system. Like a scale, with weights on either side, a person's value system must be weighted appropriately so that their life is properly balanced. For example, someone might compare their spouse to a reality TV show bride (or groom). They make painful statements about their spouse when they are triggered, perhaps about their appearance or ability to fit the role of what the person thinks they should measure up to. They subconsciously sabotage their relationship with these unrealistic expectations and set themselves up for failure by these delusions of a relationship as they perceive it yet that might not even exist in the first place!

Many times, in an effort to supposedly save the relationship they will reach out to different sources for help: new diet fads, counseling, self-help books, and more. All these things can be great but are nothing more than a drain on your finances if they are not helpful and utilized appropriately.

In my eleven years of ministry, I have seen a lot in this field. I once worked with a married couple who could not be intimate unless the woman was wearing makeup. The woman was afraid her husband would not be attracted enough to her, and sadly he feared the same.

Needless to say, they struggled with strongholds in their personal lives— pornography and lust, which were setting their unrealistic and unhealthy expectations. They could no longer just love each other or express that love in any kind of unrehearsed fashion, but instead intimacy was replaced with fantasy and performance. In this instance, the marriage was placed on one side of the scale and on the other side was pornography.

A marriage set on the scale in this fashion will never come to balance for many reasons.

The foundations of pornography include the following: performance, illusion, lies, lust, adultery, abuse, and scenarios leading to unhealthy ideas about sex, intimacy, and relationships in general. The person can never balance these ideas with the everyday challenges of marriage. In order for balance to occur, the marriage would have to be equal with the same performance, illusion, lies, lust, adultery, abuse, and unhealthy scenarios about sex, intimacy and relationships.

The only way to save a marriage when the value system is set to something as intrinsically damaging as pornography is to take the marriage off the scale. Marriage and pornography will never compete. They will never balance each other. You would have to change the foundations of one or the other for them to ever balance. Pornography has a specific definition, but marriage is a relationship built on many things, including culture and personal values. This means that ten times out of ten, pornography will define the marriage.

The only way to balance the marriage is to destroy the scale. You might need to get a new scale entirely!

While this isn't intended to be a purity talk, this is still one of the most powerful examples for this illustration.

As Christians, or even for those curious about God, his existence, and his view of creation, only one thing on the other side of the scale can bring our lives and relationships into balance.

I'm an avid lover of all things psychology and mental-health related. I will often joke about how I use my experience in counseling since I received mental health services for years before I even went into ministry. I've studied secular and faith-based psychology for many years, and let me tell you something—there's so much wisdom to be found in many amazing secular writings and techniques that could help the faith-based communities if they would just stop demonizing them. Even so, I find that secular psychology only takes people so far. With great tactics, new coping skills, and incredible wisdom, they take people to the very brink of success but, many times leave them hanging. They give them a taste of freedom and self-control but leave off the very thing that will make the pivotal change in a person's life, bringing them to balance! So what is this key element? What has the power to bring a life into true balance from the core?

It's the *truth*. Truth will bring people, marriages, relationships, and individual lives into perfect balance.

"I am the way and the truth and the life. No one comes to the Father except through me" (John 14:6, NIV).

Jesus is the way, the truth, and the life. When you place *him* on the other side of the scale, he will always bring balance!

"But whoever is united with the Lord is one with him in spirit." (1 Corinthians 6:17, NIV).

If you know Jesus as your personal Lord and Savior, the thought of you and Christ as one spirit might be overwhelming, but you must come to this realization. He is safe to put on the other side of the scale. He is not distant, far-off, and looking down on you but is instead *one* with you, working inside you. You do not balance with Christ because of anything you have done but because of all that He has done. When you finally realize these truths, you will find the one and only solution to your life and become balanced in all areas.

One of the most effective ways of putting him on your scale in place of everything else that will now yield you freedom, love, or truth is learning who he is and what it means for him to truly work inside you.

This might be a journey, but if you think about an addict and how long they take to learn the ins and outs of their addictions on the other side of their scale in place of Jesus, the journey is in both directions. Time will pass. Your life will move forward. You will grow older. Seasons will change. But how will you spend your life? Will you be using your time to fix things that are constantly out of balance? Do you find that the practices you've executed previously do not actually bring you freedom but instead are survival tactics? Do you feel that you can't grasp true change in your life? It's time to get *shift* done!

The scale is personal to *you*. Your scale will not look like my scale, but what balances your scale is not unique to you. The things you have struggled with or competed with are not solely yours. People often carry an entrapping mindset that their problems are unique to them. Whatever you have faced, *someone* has faced before you, has made a change in a positive direction, and has overcome. The only defeated people are those who believe their issues cannot be solved because they are powerless to overcome them and that nobody could ever understand their pain. This is wrong. Someone on the planet has been through what you have been through. If nothing else, this truth should help you know that you are not alone. Victory is attainable and available; it just might not always look how you expect it to look, come when or how you expect it to come, and it might make you change in ways you didn't realize you need to. This simply means be *open*! Be open to the Holy Spirit and what he might have for you as you read this book and travel this journey. Be patient and graceful with yourself and enjoy the process.

Chapter 1: Reclaiming Purpose

We've all had a horrible ordeal—a dark night of the soul—at least once as adults. Life happens. Much occurs that's outside our control that can really rock our world.

I remember my dark night as if it were yesterday. At 3:00 a.m., I was in bed alone, screaming at the top of my lungs. I woke up like this. I wasn't quite sure what reality was, but once I found out, I didn't want to accept it. Sleeping alone isn't that unusual for me as my husband is a traveling minister, but this night, the room felt like the hollow of an isolated cave. The darkness was darker than I can describe by simply saying the lights were out. It was the darkest dark I think I have ever seen. I woke from my nightmare to find myself living in it. It was real, and I couldn't separate my dreams from my reality.

I was screaming, like a thunderous roar from such a deep place within, "*Nooooo!*" It felt as if a creature was being let out from inside me. What was that creature? It was trauma.

Hours earlier, my four-year-old son, newly potty-trained, had been diagnosed with cancer. He lay lifeless in a hospital bed as the nurses rushed to insert all kinds of tubes and needles into his body to take blood, give blood, receive transfusions, and run massive amounts of tests. My husband stayed with him overnight at the hospital, and I took my other children home with some people from my church who came to assist how they could. As soon as I put my newborn and toddler to bed, I lay there in bed crying— deep heavy cries out to God, not understanding a thing that was happening.

I eventually passed out, exhausted from my intense sobbing sessions but woke up screaming, "*Nooooo!*" at the top of my lungs. "*Don't take my baby! Take me, please don't take him!*"

I never thought I would pray for cancer,

but I was so desperate that the time that I would have taken anything so that my children didn't have to suffer.

You see, we didn't even have an official diagnosis for twenty-four hours. I asked questions like, "What kind of cancer does he have?" and "Is he going to make it?"

I expected them to undeniably confirm his survival chances, but to my shock and horror they could offer me nothing for weeks.

"Sorry, ma'am. We cannot guarantee anything at this time." They gave me no other answers.

In my perfectionism a lot of attention came to the surface about my son's leukemia diagnosis. My husband and I knew we would have to present this news to our worldwide family in Christ, but how? We were already asking for prayer, and many were praying, but how would we present tell everyone that the doctors had just informed us that our son had the 'c' word?

We decided from the very beginning that we were going to present this victoriously. We looked up other kid's pages and sadly found many. Childhood cancer isn't rare, as it turns out, but most of the pages were "Pray for So and So" or "Amy's Fight Against Cancer." (I did not really see an Amy, but I did not want to name any real pages.) So many of the stories were terrifying. We didn't want to speak that this was going to be a fight, so we decided not to.

We prayed and talked for twenty-four hours in the midst of our own pain and trauma that was trying to creep in. We came up with the perfect name to share our journey with the world to remind everyone—including us—that this horrible disease our son was diagnosed with had already been defeated.

We called our page and hashtag #VictoryForTitus.

We knew that we would have victory, and regardless of how that victory would manifest, we knew even more the power of our *thoughts* and our *words*! This wasn't my first time dealing with something traumatic, but it was certainly the hardest thing I had ever experienced.

I am real and raw about my emotions during this process because I received so many compliments over the years for "how well we handled things." Many people told me, "I don't know what I would do if I were you." That's true. You don't know what you would do if you were me. Our pain might not be the same, but that makes your pain and my pain no less valid. It makes the pain you experience worth feeling and working through. While I would never wish this or similar situations on anyone and would do anything to keep it from happening again, the growth that came from this has taken me to places in maturity I never even dreamed possible.

The fact that you will run into situations in life that rock your entire world is not a chance. This will definitely happen at least once in your life, and when it does, it doesn't mean you did anything whatsoever to deserve it. It's a fact of life, and it just means you are human.

How you react in the midst of the shock of it all doesn't mean you don't have the endurance to run the race set before you either. I woke up screaming in my sleep night after night, but every day found strength to get dressed, work out, take care of my children and be there for my son during his intense treatment protocol. It was not easy, and we were just settling down when my world began to crumble around me. Not long before my son's diagnosis, I was in the middle of writing my first book. We were working very hard in ministry and really felt we were making an impact for the kingdom. We have always been hard workers, but we were receiving massive revelation about identity, had just moved across the country, and were in the middle of getting settled in our new life when everything went spinning out of control. We held onto faith, of course, even when we felt like we were being catapulted into a universe without any gravity to ground us.

At first, I was extremely concerned

about everyone else around me who knew what I was going through. I was concerned that someone was so worried about me that they wouldn't be able to relate to me anymore. I did everything I could to show that our family was not unreachable. I attended church the very next Sunday while my husband and son were in the hospital.

Regardless of my attempts, life started to fall apart all around me. Relationships became really strange. I dealt with massive rejection and betrayal. For months, our two youngest children (at the time) were not allowed at the hospital due to a flu ban while my oldest child was in isolation with zero immunity.

As if all that weren't enough, he had a severe allergy and reaction to one of the chemotherapy drugs that almost killed him. The only possible solution to continue protocol were leg injections that when administered, felt like burning fire. These had to be administered every other day, two weeks on and two weeks off, for months. I can't describe the torment of holding my son down, knowing what we were putting into him, and hearing his screams. I wanted to leave my body.

In the height of it all, I started to break. I wasn't sure how I felt about anything or anyone anymore. I felt so alone and started to see holographic images of myself hanging around my house. This is an intense description, but it is absolutely true. I called my husband and cried, describing what I was seeing. I pleaded with him, asking, "I know I don't want to die. Why am I seeing this?"

I have never publicly talked about these attacks I experienced through the first year of my son's treatments in such great detail. I know that many people go through severe trauma and feel alone. I want to reassure you that you are *not* alone.

If you've read my first book, *Daddy Issues a New Life*, I go into great detail of my experience with mental illness, abuse, mental health institutions, and so on. I know exactly what symptoms of mental illness are. What was different about this experience from those previous symptoms is that I could finally see that this was an attack on our family and on our lives.

You see, I still loved my family, and it was so terrible to experience seeing these images of myself, because I fought to survive. I didn't want to die. I wanted my son well, and I needed to be alive and healthy to take care of him and my other children.

I finally saw that this was actually a spirit of depression and suicide attacking my mind and not just some kind of resurfacing of mental illness from the past.

I was at rock bottom. Many believe that people are a sum of their choices, but I beg to differ. I had been in ministry for eight years when my son was diagnosed. Rob and I had an incredible marriage (still do)! We dedicated our kids to the Lord from the womb and named them all Biblical names. I had home births. We even went vegan for six months before he was diagnosed. I did everything I knew how to be the best heavenly daughter, wife, and mother I could be.

I didn't make a decision that brought me to this place. This was clear destruction attacking my life. Once I realized this, it still had no power to dictate how my life would be played out from then on.

See, any type of spirits can mimic an attack, but they are defeated at the cross. The only way they can have power to keep you down is to convince you that you have no power over them. While I could accept that my family had been attacked, I was no longer going to allow this enemy to destroy my life. I might have had to watch my son live most of his childhood from a hospital bed or clinic, and I might have lost a lot of relationships who didn't know how to deal with what I was going through, but I did not have to let this stop me from what God was calling me to do.

It took day by day of looking at myself in the mirror with bloodshot eyes and saying, "Millie, you know the plans God has for your family, and today is the first day to restart that plan. Nothing will get in your way from being the motivator and natural go-getter that you are!"

And while it took years and tons of healing to process all that had happened, I was able to let God rekindle the fires he had placed inside me from birth. I was able to reclaim my purpose, and I knew that I didn't want our family to be known as "the family with the son who had cancer" but instead as "the family who tramples on snakes and scorpions and impacts the kingdom of heaven here on earth!"

Along the way, I picked up many tools to motivate myself to get back on my feet, get my family healthy, refocus on freedom and positive thoughts through healing, finish writing my first book, and move forward with the plans God had for our lives.

I pray that as you read this book, you are able to take time and activation to truly implement some, if not all, of these principles. I know they will take you from the depths of whatever you have been through, are going through, or might go through in the future to the manifest destiny God has for your life!

Chapter 2: PCH

My husband and I have this little code language. We've been in full time ministry for eleven years now, and in that time, we've done much research and many personal development studies. After all, we did not come from homes with any kind of entrepreneurial background. It didn't take us long to figure out that certain things were holding us back from reaching our full potential. Growth and maturity became a *decision* for us, but it wouldn't come naturally. We first invested both time and money into developing ourselves and one of the first things I personally learned that was holding us back was...

Negativity!

Negativity will hold you back. Negativity will repel people, positivity, opportunity, motivation, passion, and growth!

Growing up in the northeast United States, I never imagined such a thing. Everything was negative from inside jokes to our perspective on life. My husband and I were both Christians because of having major radical experiences that pointed us to Jesus. Even more, we put key biblical principles into practice in our daily lives, living *completely* by faith and asking total strangers if we could pray for them and believe for miracles right in the streets. Although this was great, we still did not recognize our negative attitude and perspective. Perhaps it was cultural, I'm not sure.

That's just the thing. Sometimes what holds us back isn't something bad or sinful that is choking us. It can be something as sly and passive as negativity.

I developed a new lifelong quest to change the areas of my mind and heart that would almost naturally pick up negativity and focused on somehow flipping around this natural pattern. I decided to start with my thoughts and even how I talked with my husband behind closed doors. If someone got to me, I really wanted to talk about it and process it. This isn't necessarily bad, but my new mission was to talk positively as much as possible about my experiences in general. To do this, I didn't have to be dishonest in this process, I just had to change my perspective.

I realized that in so much of my selective memory, I had trained myself to not only focus on the negative parts of my experiences but to almost completely disregard the positive ones. Yes, negative things were happening, but positive things were happening too. I could most definitely address the negative as needed because sometimes we *do* need to process those things, but I realized in choosing to remain negative, I missed out on so many blessings that the positive experiences offered.

For example, I could spend the day sleeping in, having a great breakfast, listening to my child say something so profound that melted my heart into a big, huge puddle, and celebrating with ice cream together, but then one person might cut me off in traffic and the day's focus completely shifted!

I often said the following when people drove crazily. "These people have no regard for human life!" Things like this especially got to me once I had children in the car because I couldn't understand how people could be so careless when operating a machine at eighty miles per hour with the potential to destroy other's families.

I could definitely address those things and point out their lack of regard, but if I dwelled too much on it, it could steal the joy and positivity from the day I was enjoying just moments before that negative encounter.

So instead I began to focus my efforts on...

Positivity!

As I reviewed the day with my spouse, I began to look for the positives. Negativity in your life is like a disease in a sense. You actually have to overcome it. You will actually have to intentionally look for the positives and choose to focus on and speak about those as highlights.

I began to seek out more positive environments and relationships. To this day, I tend to drift away from negative conversations. I don't love negative people less, but I want to keep my surroundings positive. Some people truly enjoy being negative. If you are trying to overcome negativity, you will have to learn to lean into positivity. When you can't influence these atmospheres for the positive, you will need to learn when it's time to let go of those relationships so that you can maintain your own focus on positivity.

At times, you will feel that you should reach out to people who are negative, but while you are in the process of renewing and retraining your own mind, you will especially need to be mindful of keeping some space between you and these negative environments.

As I retrained my mind from being negative and pessimistic, I began to notice other things. For instance, I had not only suffered negativity in talking about other people but also in how I talked about myself.

For whatever reason, I picked up this subconscious belief that confidence was prideful and that somehow dumbing myself down would be humble. Imagine that! If you've read my first book, *Daddy Issues a New Life*, you might understand where this subconscious belief might have stemmed from. I was not allowed to think very highly of myself growing up, and to top it off, being a positive, confident person was labeled as being fake and prideful. By the time I reached adulthood, I could not ever accept even one single compliment. If someone said anything nice about me, I didn't even believe them. Now I wasn't a bad person, but I just thought did not believe I should think *good* of myself. There's a mental game!

By putting into practice my new positive perspectives, I realized that I couldn't possibly go on believing this terrible way about myself while trying to move forward into being a positive person. I had to face the fact that there were positive things of not only the world around me, but also *in* me. I had to see the best things about my personality, appearance, and character and admit to myself that there was good in me. In admitting these good things about me, my definition of humility vs. pride changed dramatically and, in fact, reversed! I began to believe different things about myself!

When I started to believe those positive things about myself, other areas of my life changed as well. I carried myself differently. I talked about myself differently, and therefore the way I presented myself changed overall. I no longer allowed people to treat me negatively or even joke about the person I was in a negative tone. I started to believe I had value and worth. This new perspective was slowly changing my life, and I learned that it wasn't a fight to get others to see me as positive. In my thought/action evaluation and processing, I learned that people basically believe much of what you tell them about yourself! This isn't to say that you have to gloat about your talents and abilities, but this relates to how you refer to yourself. Even when someone made a lighthearted joke— was the tone more positive or negative? People talked about me in the same way I referred to myself.

One of the ways this was most evident was when someone paid me a compliment. My first reaction was to shy away, look to the ground, and mumble, "No . . . " or "Whatever . . . . " But as my patterns changed, I learned to confidently smile and say, "Thank you." I might even say nothing at all and just receive it. I started to believe in myself. I began to trust who I was. I was developing a true...

Confidence and Humility!

Through confidence, I started to discover the safety of not needing to over-promote who I was. I did not need to overcome negativity by swinging to the other side of the pendulum, boasting in my talents, abilities, character, and quality. Instead the healthy knowledge I sought out brought me to a very stable middle ground that helped me balance believing in my potential without boasting about it. This part of the puzzle was essential for keeping me grounded and focused. You see, others don't want to hear an earful of how great even the most talented and amazing person is. The balance between believing in and not boasting was not a hard journey for me to travel but for many it is. There I began to focus on the last piece of my personal adventure with self-discovery.

Confidence, however, is not to be confused with false humility but is *true* fearless humility. Confidence is knowing who you really are and displaying your call without fear of labels or stigmas or rejection. I heard a teacher once talk about the difference between translations when referring to the verse, "avoid all appearance of evil." (See 1 Thessalonians 5:22.) This verse is actually translated incorrectly and the more accurate translations say, "Avoid all *forms* of evil." He went on to say how we tiptoe around doing completely unnecessary things to "avoid all appearance of evil" when that scripture is not even translated correctly. What we are really doing is walking in fear of suspicion: suspicion of pride and suspicion of sin. We neglect to recognize that we are just plain walking in *fear*! Once again, I can't stress the importance of not doing this. We shouldn't walk in fear on any level! We need to walk w i t h *kingdom* confidence and instead of kicking our shoe when someone compliments us, we should actually just receive it. Instead of apologizing for things we didn't do, just move on.

I've always struggled with saying, "I'm sorry!" all the time. This is not humility or confidence! This is fear disguised as humility, weakness disguised as meekness. This is the exact opposite of kingdom confidence and is not meant for us. I might add that these things are actually, medically verified as dangerous for our bodies to hold on to. Stress releases toxic hormones into our bodies and triggers diseases that we probably don't even know are linked to our lack of confidence.

This tiny recipe began my journey to learning self-improvement. These three keys were foundational to everything I would learn about being successful, staying motivated, and maintaining focus throughout the rest of my life. I shared this journey with my husband, and when he flew out to speak at a new event or church around the country, I reminded him of our little key phrase, "PCH". Both he and I knew exactly what it meant: Positivity, Confidence, and Humility. These would be the foundation and forefront of our every agenda. I also learned that others were expecting this from us as leaders and guides to people on their journeys. It wouldn't be the answer to every dilemma, and it wouldn't skyrocket us into success, but it would be the building blocks to all of those things. I knew that if we could master this concept, we could master anything and help others do the same!

Ask yourself:

Have I been in seasons outside of my control where I was surrounded by negativity that was difficult to combat? Has this affected how I viewed situations or how I responded? Has this been a blockade to having a positive mindset? List your strategy for changing your mindset (setting your mind on things above).

_____
_____
_____
_____
_____
_____
_____
_____
_____
_____

Have you taken steps to remain confident without falling into the traps of false humility, which is actually pride? List some positive qualities about yourself that you can be confident in without fear of sounding too prideful:

_____
_____
_____
_____
_____

_____

_____

_____

_____

In what ways in the past have you thought that you were actually "avoiding the appearance of evil" when you were really walking in fear of other people's opinions? How might you better view this scripture to avoid walking in fear but instead walk in confidence and true humility?

_____

_____

_____

_____

_____

_____

_____

_____

_____

Some notes about 1 Thessalonians 5:22 from Hans Deventer and Dennis R. Bratcher: (Christian Resource Institute - http://www.crivoice.org/appearance.html)

Most Protestants, especially those in the evangelical traditions, place great value on Scripture as the basis for developing theology or taking ethical stands. For them, Scripture is important in providing guidelines for how to live in the world as God's people. However, with this emphasis on Scripture also comes the responsibility of careful attention to issues of interpretation. It is all too easy to slip into the comfortable but irresponsible habit of using Scripture to support ideas or positions that are personal opinions, social mores, or the practices of a particular culture at a certain time and place in history.

Sometimes this occurs simply by ignoring any interpretation except that which produces a desired result. Sometimes, however, it is the result of misunderstanding the biblical text, from faulty translation, or from not knowing enough about the biblical text, either in terms of word meanings, the historical or cultural background of the text, or the larger context in which a passage is set. This emphasizes the need for careful and thoughtful attention to those features of any biblical text before using that text as the basis for doctrine or ethical positions, or in developing personal applications of a passage.

One simple example of how faulty translation, combined with uncritical use of that translation within a certain cultural and historical context, can lead to serious misapplication of a passage of Scripture can be seen in 1 Thessalonians 5:22.

In the NRSV, the verse is translated: "abstain from every form of evil." A literal translation of the Greek might be: "from every form of evil be abstaining."

However, in the KJV, the translation most widely used in the English-speaking world until the mid 20th-century, the verse is translated: "abstain from every appearance of evil."

The differences in translation center around the meaning of the Greek term *"eidous."* This word only occurs five times in the Greek New Testament, although it is a frequent term in the Greek translation of the Old Testament (the Septuagint), occurring there 58 times. According to Thayer

(*Thayer's Greek-English Lexicon*), as well as Bauer, Ardt, and Gingrich (*A Greek-English Lexicon of the New Testament*), this term has two main meanings:

1) the external or outward appearance, form, figure, shape. It occurs with this meaning in Luke 3:22 ("in bodily form"), 9:29 ("the appearance of his face"), and John 5:37 ("you have never heard his voice or seen his form"). Similarly, it can also mean sight or seeing, as in 2 Corinthians 5:7 ("we walk by faith, not by sight").

2) form, kind. This is not the usual meaning of the term in most of the Septuagint. However, it does occur with this meaning in classical Greek, as well as in some of the apocryphal writings (for example, Sirach 23:16: "two kinds of individuals multiply sins, and a third incurs wrath . . ."). Bauer lists this meaning for 1 Thessalonians 5:22: "from every kind of evil."

It is easy to see why the KJV translators, and many of the older translations into Dutch, English, French and German, used a term equivalent to "appearance" to translate *"eidous"* since that was the most common meaning in most of the biblical texts. However, as anyone who works with languages knows, the most used meaning of any term in a language does not dictate that it must always mean that.

Chapter 3: Distractions and Focus

One of the biggest tools in maintaining motivation is developing focus. If you are a naturally focused person like I am, you might be fairly good at eliminating distractions that interfere with your focus.

Assessing and Identifying Distraction

The more I cut out distractions around me, the more space and creativity I find. Distractions can be found even among the good things in our lives, but if they are inhibiting productivity and preventing us from moving in the direction of our passions, they can become a roadblock. They can be tricky to spot because they gain power when we are weak or tired and craving comfort or enjoyment. We have to learn to gauge the need of our goal in order to assess and identify exactly what to consider a distraction.

For example, music has been a big part of my life since I was eleven years old. My cousin came to live with us, and I took up the flute that she had owned. She was not interested in playing, so she said I could start. I quickly joined my school's free lessons, moved on to the school band, and was drum majorette of the marching band as a junior in high school. Learning this skill took many hours of focused study and paying close attention to each precise note, beat, and count. I later came to appreciate learning an instrument at such a young age. It taught me the amount of focus I would need to excel at anything. When you set aside the proper time to completely learn a new skill, you will advance quickly. By the time I joined a church of my own accord at fourteen, I was drawn quickly to singing and the worship team. Since then, I have been on several worship teams. One of my main desires from my early ministry days was to play an instrument that was focal to leading a small worship band of my own. Though I learned many basic guitar and piano chords, I never really took off in that direction. Though this is still a dream in my heart, I have now developed a passion for writing. Anyone can set aside time to do a little of several things they have passion for. I knew I was going to start writing books! You need focus, lots of time, and peace of mind to produce a well-written book. As I write this paragraph, I see the guitar I desire to play in the same room, and even though it is a passion of mine, it can easily distract me from hitting the deadlines I have set for each book I have yet to write. I'm not saying that one is more important than the other, but for *me*, God has placed things in my heart to write at this moment. Since I'm very focused, I prefer not to be chasing several goals at one time.

The main idea I'm trying to get across is that even some deep passions and desires can become distractions when we spend more time on them than we should in a season led by a specific goal and purpose. Sometimes we think that a distraction is a bill collector calling at the wrong time. Yes, that,too, is a distraction. But distractions can also be positive things in our life in the wrong season that drain too much of our time and energy. I do believe season will come when I focus more time on the guitar so that I can pick it up for leisure here and there, but my faith, family, ministry, and writing are my priorities. Being a mom of five leaves me little room for more passions than what I already have, and so much of my focus *has* to be budgeted.

Distractions can be beneficial when managed.

Mindless distractions can be helpful and even *necessary*! (After all I wrote in the last paragraphs, I'm sure I've confused you!) I'm not saying *all* distractions are bad. As I've already described, some of my well-meaning, out-of-season passions can be a distraction, but when managed well I can still enjoy them at my leisure. Some distractions help relax us in a season with intense pressure or workloads. I have a few default distractions that are not like my desire to lead worship in any sense. Beneficial distractions can actually be mindless activities you enjoy. For a distraction to be beneficial during a season of intensity, the distraction should not be pointed to any other area of potential in your life. For example, learning to play the guitar would not be a mindless distraction for me as I have goals that would push me to grow in my skills, thus adding more intensity to my life where it is not most beneficial.

Some of my favorite mindless distractions, for example, are a simple app game on my iPhone called "Wheel of Fortune," a book of word searches, or Sudoku. I find when I spend time on those areas I enjoy, my mind releases the stress of being in work mode all day every day, and my productivity skyrockets because when it is to time to focus, I can focus more clearly. You do need to set limits and boundaries with these miniature mind vacations. I'll often say, "Okay, I will play a few games of Wheel of Fortune on my phone while I nurse my baby, but when he is finished, the phone goes back on the charger and I go back to focus!" This works well because I've set limits for myself.

As long as I've built the trust within myself to listen, I can become recharged during those moments of enjoyment and be ready for the rest of the day.

You need to develop a trust within yourself.

Talk to yourself! That's right, you read that correctly! That taboo old wives' tale that anyone who talks to themselves must be crazy is just that—crazy! (If you answer yourself, however, they say that's when you are truly crazy . . . just kidding!) Some studies show that people who talk to themselves are often more intelligent. In reality, it doesn't matter if you really do talk to yourself out loud or not, but get to know who you are and begin to trust yourself. I will touch on this more in the chapters on identity and culture ahead. You will build that trust through personal reflection and a keen sense of identity. This will go much deeper than knowing your own personal preferences. You will also learn the depths of your passions, the limits of your patience, and your potential for growth. All of this is essential when you sit down exhausted at the end of the day and know that you have already decided that you're going to work toward that something great in your heart. In all reality, you are just too tired or the brightness of that once-blazing passion is starting to grow dim with distractions and/or the mundane tasks of plain ol' life! In those moments, you need to trust yourself to say, "I need a break. I need a mindless distraction or rest." That trust within you will allow you to take a half hour of mindless distraction or even a complete day of rest without completely falling off the bandwagon and losing your focus all together. You don't want to turn this into a habit where one day of rest turns into two, which then turns into two years. This can so easily happen. That's why it's important to assess the types of distractions in your life, how you will manage them, and build the trust within yourself to actually manage them appropriately.

Ask yourself:

What are some great passions in my life that
I want to accomplish? (Make a list)

_____

_____

_____

_____

_____

_____

_____

Of those passions, what are the top one or
two that are most important?

_____

_____

_____

_____

_____

_____

_____

_____

What are some mindless distractions I could
enjoy in moderation? Examples might include

games on your phone, crafts, hobbies, television, movies, or even taking a walk.

_____

_____

_____

_____

_____

_____

_____

Can I trust myself to stay focused and committed to my passions by managing my distractions? If so, how?

_____

_____

_____

_____

_____

_____

_____

_____

_____

_____

_____

You can't "make" time!

A lot of people in the health-and-fitness industry hound people to make time. As a fitness enthusiast myself, I can appreciate their perspective to a point. I might have even promoted the same exact idea a time or two. "You don't have the time to work out? Nobody has the time to work out! You *make* time to work out." That's just the thing. You can't make time! You are not God, and you absolutely cannot make time. You can only give the time you already have. I like this saying a lot better. "We all have the same twenty-four hours in a day to work with." This is far more accurate. All of us have twenty-four hours every single day of our lives. Some of our commitments require a great deal of those hours in certain seasons, but once we decide the order of importance regarding our commitments and passions, we can learn to manage our time more effectively. All that we can do with our time is manage it. At times, I tried to follow the idea of making time. All I really did was steal time from something else that was important or even essential to me. For instance, when I added too many things into my day, trying to be superwoman, I just stayed up later at night and got up earlier, not realizing that I was making a lifestyle and bad habit of sowing my time for sleep into another category that was much less important. I couldn't excel in that because sleep is a high priority in achieving successful productivity. Even though I thought I was making time for other important things, I was becoming less successful because I was sowing too much time into things that were less of a priority in my life.

You have to come to the place where you truly own your time. Time is a seed that's yours to either sow or spend. Spending time alludes to debt, and your time belongs to someone or something else, but sowing seeds of time into fruitful ground will yield a plentiful harvest. This is not only because you took ownership of your time, but because you did it with the right heart. It was not born out of duty but born out of purpose. In this, you've designated your biggest asset: your time. We can't play God and act like we can make time, but we can be real about the time that we have and steward it correctly.

Motivation and focus are everything. To become or remain a focused person does not mean you need to cut *all* distractions from your life. It simply means you need to identify what you need to *focus* on, what is a *distraction*, and what kinds of distraction they are (distractions designed for a different season, mindless distractions, or just plain old telemarketer calls). Then divide up your seeds of time accordingly. I highly suggest focusing on only one or two *major* life passions at a time for maximum effectiveness. Identifying these things and putting a plan of action in place can greatly increase your motivation to stick with your goals for the long run.

Chapter 4:

Discovering Your Passion by Knowing Your Identity

One of the most important journeys you will embark on in life is discovering who you are. Most people are searching for elements in life that give them purpose and drive, but once you have that scope of your identity, everything you love and desire will flow from you. One of the things I've learned in raising children is that you really do not have to force them to take an interest in things. Sometimes we want our children to like what we liked as a child, but to no avail.

Children have a mind all their own, and they are usually not afraid to express themselves! As children, however, they are not focused on their identity. Most children that I have met who come from healthy homes have a built-in identity system. They know who they belong to. They know they are a son or a daughter and who their parents are. They are well aware of their nature and have a basic understanding of their cultural surroundings. They look for intricacies in their appearance by looking to their father and mother. As adulthood approaches and as they learn a new way of thinking that requires added responsibilities and knowledge, they start seeing the faults and flaws of their parents and venture on the journey to start providing for themselves. If they, at that point, don't already have a keen sense of identity, they often travel many lonely roads in search of it.

Discovering your identity is foundational and should be developed during your early childhood years, expanding in maturity as you grow. But if you have not had that opportunity, it is never too late. Every one of your dreams and passions is going to stem from the core of who you are—the key is knowing who that is in the first place.

Who are you?

Who are you and what are you drawn to? The technical definition of an identity might include some surface results regarding a simple name, heritage, or genetic factor, but as you dig deeper into your identity, I challenge you to search out your heart, character, convictions, and desires. What is something you've wanted for a long time?

Here's some more clues to consider. I don't consider comparisons to be beneficial, but if you ever have compared yourself to anyone and felt defeated in some area, what was it in? Although comparisons in relationships can lead directly to jealousy and envy—which is a recipe for disaster—our past struggles with comparisons can give us insight into what we truly desire! When others excel in our own area of interest, a true heart of success will mature out of that jealousy and frustration and learn to glean and celebrate the giftings of others.

You might be reflecting on the questions I just asked you in the past couple of paragraphs, but I can tell you some inevitable truths about yourself that are foundational. The Word gives us tons of scriptures regarding identity and the fruit that knowing your identity has in a believer's life. These are key to functioning in and through your identity.

Above all else, you are a child of God. This is not just your identity since your identity is the unique characteristics and qualities you carry. But the knowledge that you are a child of God means that you know your very nature and the new creation that you are. "Well, how do I even know that I qualify for that? How do I know that this is my nature or that I am indeed a new creation?"

"Yet to all who did receive him, to those who believed in his name, he gave the right to become children of God" (John 1:12 NIV).

If you've responded to the free gift of salvation Jesus poured out on the cross more than two thousand years ago, then you know that you are a child of God! Does this mean all will be good and perfect from that moment on? Not necessarily. Life is a journey, but you have access to every fruit of the Spirit found in Galatians 5:22–23!

"He predestined us for adoption to sonship through Jesus Christ, in accordance with his pleasure and will" (Ephesians 1:5 NIV).

Adopting you wasn't just some duty of Jesus but was in accordance with his pleasure and will! You are not only a fulfillment of His pleasure and will, but he predestined this for you the entire time. You do not have to fight for your nature in him, just simply receive it. Sometimes receiving is hard. Personally my love language is not gifts or giving gifts. (If you've ever read *The 5 Love Languages* by Gary Chapman, you will know what I'm referencing here.) In fact, the love language of gifts is most certainly last on my list, and because of this, receiving can actually be difficult for me and many others who are wired similarly.

The gospel, which means good news, is good news because you can't even begin to understand your original value and produce the incredible fruit of it until you simply receive the fact that you have been predestined for adoption to sonship through Jesus Christ.

"But I know many who have good fruit in their lives and are not even believers!" Just imagine when they do come to receive and believe the truth of who they are in Christ. I know very well that the gifts and calling are without repentance. (See Romans 11:29.) This means that, believer or not, God has placed some great gifts inside of people based on his belief about them. God believes amazing things about you and placed great gifts inside you according to his belief and all of that is in accordance with his pleasure and will. Whether you like it or not, that's how he feels about you and that is what he has done for you. I believe that the manifestations of these things are nowhere near the scale of their full potential until you do receive these things by faith. Your heavenly identity if your true identity! Living from your heavenly identity will transform your identity on earth.

"Accept one another, then, just as Christ accepted you, in order to bring praise to God" (Romans 15:7 NIV).

When you come to know and believe what Christ has said about you and how he has accepted you, you will begin to manifest that same love and acceptance to others. It will flow out of you, which is purely a side effect of knowing your identity in him!

Becoming an influential person on any platform requires a genuine love for people. You cannot wear a mask, but that will take complete openness on your journey to receiving his love and acceptance for you. It's easier to love others when you know you are loved. More than just being loved in some sort of one-dimensional reality is, of course, far deeper dimensions of understanding this capacity of love and acceptance. The more you dive into the love God has for you, this will undoubtedly manifest through you and into the lives of those around you. Love and acceptance are contagious like wildfire and explosive enough to bring change to your community and even to the world by just starting with you!

"For in Christ all the fullness of the Deity lives in bodily form, and in Christ you have been brought to fullness. He is the head over every power and authority" (Colossians 2:9–10 NIV).

If I walked up to you today and told you that the *fullness* of God lives inside of you and in *him* you have been brought to fullness, could you really wrap your mind around that thought? This amazing treasure dwells within us! This is such a deep truth to try and comprehend, and it's okay if you need to mediate on this scripture to fully digest all the possibilities of meanings. If I were to gloat in the victory of the kingdom of God over darkness, I would admit that I love how the Amplified Bible dissects this particular verse:

"For in Him all the fullness of Deity (the Godhead) dwells in bodily form [completely expressing the divine essence of God]. And in Him you have been made complete [achieving spiritual stature through Christ], and He is the head over all rule and authority [of every angelic and earthly power]."

The word fullness in this passage is *pleroma* and is described by Wikipedia as follows:

Pleroma (Greek πλήρωμα) generally refers to the totality of divine powers (https://en.wikipedia.org/wiki/Pleroma).

This is a big concept to fully understand and digest, which might take some of us our entire lives. When you start to see that God is not some external, far-off being who leaves the moment you do something wrong and then comes close to you as soon as you do something right, you will begin to realize that he is embodied inside your very being. All of the totality of divine powers he offers over each and every other principality and authority manifest from *within* you through him! This is foundational but so intricate to understanding your capabilities as part of and from within your identity.

65

"But whoever is united with the Lord is one with him in spirit" (1 Corinthians 6:17 NIV).

There is no separation between you and your Creator God! Once you receive that unity with him, you are *one* with him. If this doesn't change your perspective as to how you see yourself, I'm not quite sure what will. Keep meditating on these scriptures and truths until you grasp this reality. Dive deeper and deeper into understanding these vital words!

"For we know that our old self was crucified with him so that the body ruled by sin might be done away with, that we should no longer be slaves to sin." (Romans 6:6 NIV).

The nature that you formerly carried is no longer part of you and has no say in who you become. Your past failures have no bearing on your future success. You'll notice in the world—and even among Christians—that when someone fails in an area, we want to crucify any hope for their future. This is not the heart of God nor is it in our DNA as believers. Our heart should break when we see someone manifest anything other than the reality of their identity according to the kingdom of heaven! You'll notice that once you begin to have grace for yourself, you will also have grace for others. If you struggle in a certain area in your life, remind yourself that your old nature is crucified and you are not ruled by that nature any longer. Instead you are now a slave to righteousness.

"So God created mankind in his own image, in the image of God he created them; male and female he created them" (Genesis 1:27 NIV).

My darling, look in the mirror. If you don't see God there, look deeper and realize that you are created in the very image of God himself! If you've never heard this before, I can reference a million children's books with this message. It's so simple that it's one of the most common Sunday School lessons available. As you remind yourself whose image you were created in, you will remember whose image you will manifest.

67

"Before I formed you in the womb I knew you, before you were born I set you apart; I appointed you as a prophet to the nations" (Jeremiah 1:5 NIV).

We can see the heart God has when forming and designing a human in this Old Testament scripture. He seemed to have a specific strategy—no human was knit together by accident. If you've ever knit anything in your life, you will notice that it is extremely difficult—in fact, it's impossible—to knit something by accident. Knitting is a very tedious job. You have to count stitch by stitch and calculate perfectly to form the design. The way God designs a human and the heart behind his effort and strategy cannot be mistaken or overlooked and is every bit as applicable to the New Testament as to the Old. You were created with that very same intentionality!

(Side note: If you have been told or believed the lie that you were a mistake or accident, please take time to meditate on Jeremiah 29:11 and on Psalm 139. After you fully accept God's specific plan to develop a human as described in these scriptures, you will come to the conclusion that even if people in your life have rejected you, that is absolutely no reflection on how God views you!)

This type of predestination is more than a set path Jesus set out for you but is instead far more personal. This goes much deeper than the typical "You are here for a reason" message. He knew the inner workings of your heart before your physical heart was even created! He carefully planned out every fiber of your being and identity with precision before anyone on the planet knew you. He appointed you with all those beautiful gifts and callings he instilled into you. You are beyond special; you are uniquely, divinely planned out and purposed for great things!

"Now you are the body of Christ, and each one of you is a part of it" (1 Corinthians 12:27 NIV).

By this point, I know you are absorbing the idea that you are a very special and loved creation, but take a moment to view this from a drone perspective. There is deep greatness and mystery inside us that extends far beyond what we could see with our physical eyes. We now have a bird's-eye view that we are part of something so big and so great—a body.

Like a flood of creatures, we inhabit the planet. As believers, we are one body. When we look down at a pile of ants and observe them, you can see them move and function as a whole unit. That is how we are as a body of believers. Sometimes other believers injure us, and we like to think that because we are the Body of Christ we don't need other people. In an effort to protect ourselves, this leads us to isolation, which also potentially leads to deception about who we really are. We are in need of fellowship and must see ourselves as part of the bigger picture.

"See what great love the Father has lavished on us, that we should be called children of God! And that is what we are! The reason the world does not know us is that it did not know him. Dear friends, now we are

children of God, and what we will be has not yet been made known. But we know that when Christ appears, we shall be like him, for we shall see him as he is" (1 John 3:1–2 NIV).

So who are you? Above all else, you are first and foremost a *child* of God before you are a father, mother, sister, brother, son, or daughter. That is foundational. You are a child of the living God, and you have all the power and resources needed to accomplish what he has set before you! It might not always look how you think it should, but you will always have the opportunity and honor to manifest the kingdom of heaven right where you are. When you are hurting or misunderstood, establish yourself as *his* child!

Ask yourself:

If what I'm drawn to can give me clues about my specific giftings and the intricacies of my identity, what are some of these I've developed over the years that tell me more about myself?

_____

_____

_____

_____

_____

_____

_____

Have you ever felt rejected by someone and wondered about the purpose of your existence? Meditate on Jeremiah 29:11 (preferably with some good worship music). What is God telling you about your existence? You know it is God when what he tells you undoubtedly lines up with this scripture.

_____

_____

_____

_____

_____

_____

_____

_____

_____

_____

_____

_____

_____

_____

Last, take a moment to look at yourself from a different perspective. Act as if you are knitting something beautiful, but in reality, we are referring to your life. This will be as if you saw yourself through the eyes of God. List some amazing qualities he has put inside of you and wants you to fulfill. If this is difficult, imagine this with your child (whether or not you actually have one). God views us as his beautiful creation similar to how we view our own children with all the best hopes and desires for each of them. Write to yourself kindly and search your heart for these mysteries. Discover who you are in this quest!

_____

_____

_____

_____

Chapter 5:

It's in Your Head!

Have you ever had an idea come to you, straight to your mind? It's a moment where clarity and peace come into focus. An idea or potential opportunity arises. A road map is clear before you. You can suddenly envision the next five to then years and the success laid out in front of you, only to shrug it off and say, "Meh. That'll never happen!" If that is *not* you, that is good news! You are a clean slate, ready to start dreaming and visionating (I made up that word). If that *is* you, you might have never realized that you handed your dreams over to defeat! Everything you do starts in your head and begins as a thought or idea. Every long-term success starts with a moment's daydream. Nobody, outside of inheritance, becomes successful by accident. Even with an inheritance, a huge sum of money won't take them very far if they do not steward it correctly. You can't steward

Let's Get Shift Done!   Millie 'Joy' Radosti

something well unless you understand the concept that every good and bad outcome will first be birthed in your mind. Now I won't tell you that every time you have a great thought, nothing bad will happen when you pursue that positive idea. *Things happen!* That's just how life is. Sometimes things happen that are outside of our control but what *is* in our control is the ability to get back up and hit the ground running once again.

According to the Bible, God has given u s *incredible* powers when we focus our minds and thoughts in a certain direction. The mind is the steering wheel of the ship that is our body (actions) and life outcomes.

"For to set the mind on the flesh is death, but to set the mind on the Spirit is life and peace" (Romans 8:6 ESV).

Where we set our mind determines what we focus on. Do you feel unfocused? In a haze? Do you have trouble with time management or staying on task? Do you start things and not finish them? The scripture I noted above will key you into some insightful

76

details that, if put into practice properly, will produce amazing results.

Management

What does it mean to manage or set, as Romans 8:6 says? To set something—anything at all—it has to be in your possession. You can't set a thing down if you aren't first holding it. When you have something in your possession, you must manage the function of it, and to manage means to be in charge. You might think you've given your life over to Jesus now so that he can control your life, mind, and the outcomes of your well-meaning intentions. But this is not true. God actually gives *us* power to manage and control our own minds!

"For God gave us a spirit not of fear but of power and love and self-control" (2 Timothy 1:7 ESV).

God gave us *his* Spirit so that we have power to love unconditionally, which is supernatural, and to have what? *Self*-control! That's right! You—not God—have the control. He gave *you* control. Who do you have control over? That's right! You! This is not to say God has no power. God is still in charge but gave us dominion on the earth, including self-control over ourselves.

How a person talks might also be a clue as to what he or she is focusing on with their mind. "To set the mind on flesh is death." Those who are constantly dwelling on thoughts of the flesh, sin, and how horrible life is will constantly focus on doom and gloom and put to death the blessings around them: good relationships, their own potential, ideas, opportunities, and more. On the other hand, when a person sets their mind on the Spirit, you will see consistent, good and long-term fruit grow in their lives. A great way to test if you are managing your mind well is to look at the fruit of what you dwell on. The Bible tells us to dwell on whatever is true, honorable, just, pure, lovely, and so forth. (See Philippians 4:8.) What is the fruit of what you dwell on? Are your ventures leading to positivity? Are your outcomes leading to life? If not, it might be time to refocus. What you pursue and how you live your life is *all* in your head. Why? Because that's where it all starts. If your life is not taking you where you want to be, go back to your head, regroup, meditate on scripture, and try again!

Another way to walk in success is to start manifesting the walk before you even see success. Some studies have shown that appearance does affect productivity. People usually trust a well-dressed minister over a homeless person. Why? Does the well-dressed person (even a minister) have all the best intentions? Does a homeless person have bad intentions? Not necessarily, but much of the time, how someone presents themselves gives us insight into other areas of his or her life. I am not just referring to style but to a person taking pride in how they present themselves. This does matter in the long run. This is not to say that you can tell the intentions and motivations of a person by how they dress, but you can tell who has a lifestyle of hygiene and discipline and who is just looking for their next meal.) If you want to be a professional businessman or woman, I challenge you to buy yourself a suit jacket or maybe even a shirt with a collar. Star wearing these items as you pursue this. You are not only presenting a positive image with your appearance so that others know what to expect from you, but you are helping to set your mind toward that area of success. This practice works for me; when I dress up, I feel better about myself.

This concept of looking the part is linked to having a spirit of excellence. I don't view this as *striving* in any sense. As believers filled with the Holy Spirit, we are already equipped to function in this manner and have a spirit of excellence. Having a *spirit of excellence* means:

1. Knowing who you are. Being well aware of your identity, your nature, and your new creation reality. This includes not settling for less than the full value of what you know you're worth!
2. Maintaining health in all areas of your life. This is a fruit of knowing who you are and also an inevitable marker. This isn't to say that you will conquer all areas 100 percent of the time, but your focus will always be on making

decisions that will produce fruit in your life. You will need to eat right, exercise, pray and study, maintain your relationships, and so forth. While you might be thinking I'm referring to shifting your life in other major life areas, all of these areas of your life need to be in synch, functioning and productive to the best of your ability. Your own stress and tension—or even stress from others—will pull on your productivity in other areas.

3. Walking in your renewed mind on a consistent basis. When you see a potential opportunity, you will give it no less than your very best. You will leave things and people better than you found them. This isn't works but fruit and will flow from you because you know who you are and because you settle for nothing less. This *is* your renewed mindset!

When it comes to your identity, people will believe what you tell them about yourself and how you present yourself more than than anything else. I hear many people who are hurting refer to themselves as victims. Now we are all victims to something at least once, and I'm not trying to downplay the pain anyone has gone through. When you go through something, take *time* to go through it. If you are trying to jump into success before you've even received healing in an area you've been wronged in, it just might be time to pursue healing in that area so that you can function optimally or kingdom-ly if I can make up another word.

It's also okay to endure a season of surviving. I've done it, and I'm sure many of you have as well. These seasons are where you do what is necessary to survive. You might not even grow much, if at all, during this time. The key in those seasons is to take the time you need, and when you are ready, find ways to move forward so that you don't stay stuck in that place forever. I want to reiterate that it's absolutely okay to go through those seasons. In fact, if you've ever experienced trauma, you might be tempted to move forward quickly, but I encourage you to take the time you need to really feel what is happening, and to work through it.

I have been a part of some intense communities with many grieving parents. As such, I can say without a shadow of a doubt that grief has no time limit. People sometimes make incredibly insensitive, harsh, and ignorant comments to people going through some of the most unimaginable pain. If you are one of those people who is suffering, your grief does *not* have a time limit. You will never stop missing that person who was so special to you. Even though you can't be near them anymore, you will still grieve their existence, companionship, and love.

For the record, this does *not* disqualify you in any way. You still have all the potential in the world to make a difference, and if you can view it in this way, your success furthers the legacy of your loved one. I can say with all confidence: every good decision you make for *you* is making your loved ones proud. That's not intended to be a theological statement, but I believe it to be true. If you can receive that, it will help you make better choices, knowing that you are not dismissing the pain of losing a loved one. You are not just trying to get over them or move on without them, but you are going to make the world around you better and honoring them. You will impact the lives of others in their memory.

When you return to your season of growth after you've been healed of trauma, you will need to watch what you say about yourself.

You are no longer a victim!

You are no longer a victim of what has happened to you, so don't talk about yourself like one. The hardest thing to overcome when dealing with low self-esteem is your thoughts about yourself. Again, how you feel about yourself will start and can change right in your own mind. I've found affirmations to be extremely beneficial in this area.

If you want to completely revamp your self-image and would like some daily affirmations to hold onto, refer to the previous chapter on identity and your true nature.

Write down or print out those scriptures and say them out loud every day, but when you do, really take hold of what you are saying. Let them sink in deeply to your being!

Sample Affirmation:

My name is _____, and I am first and foremost a child of God. I was created on purpose, and my life *has* a purpose. I might not always understand what happens to me, but I know that God uses *all* things for the good for those who love him and are called according to his purpose. Though I have experienced pain and rejection, I am predestined to *love* and *acceptance*, and I carry none of my traumatic baggage from the past! I don't get over things; I work *through* them. Some people have come and gone from my life, and though I might miss them, I will carry their legacy in my heart by choosing to make a positive impact in the world! I've been a victim to some things, but this does not define me. I am *not* a victim. I am a *victor*! My mind is set on things *above*! I am always walking in and

releasing healing! My life has limitless potential. I am a *lover* of people, and my pain is transformed into testimony. My dreams are coming to pass. My relationships are blooming, and my mind is healthy. I am content with little and with much! The joy of the *Lord* is my *strength*!

It's *okay* to feel defeated! You can be brutally honest with yourself that you have made every attempt for advancement for days, moments, weeks or even for years, and nothing has worked out in your favor. You can feel as if you have given your all and that you have nothing left to give.

Stop.

Feel those feelings!

Breathe.

Process.

Take all the time you need.

I really mean this: take *all* the time you need. You are in no rush and not in a race to push yourself into a stress-induced place.

Stress is one of your biggest enemies but not if you know how to conquer it. The old saying, "work hard, play hard" is true. If you are an extremely hard worker and especially in those moments when nothing seems to be going your way, you need to know when to take a break.

What do *you* enjoy? List some activities that you personally love when you want to play hard or truly enjoy life when you are recovering from a brutal life hit or after you have worked your tail off for weeks and truly need a break. Are you building other legacies in your life outside of the machine you run? Is there a hobby or a sport you enjoy? Can you possibly pick up a new skill?

_____

_____

_____

_____

_____

_____

_____

_____

_____

_____

_____

_____

Use this space to write your own affirmation:

Chapter 6:

Relationships

I've heard so much talk over the years about alignments. Some key elements and ingredients can definitely empower amazing relationships. Relationships can push you way ahead toward your goals as you come into harmony and unison with others, or they can be one of the largest stumbling blocks you face! Much of this will depend on a few things: **the type of person you are, the type of experiences you've had in previous relationships**, and *the boundaries you now set as a result of those things.*

Knowing your identity is so important. Refer back to the section on "who you are" in the chapter about identity and nature. But even more than who you are as a person, who do others perceive you to be? How do you deal with those around you? This is where you might find it extremely helpful to invest in the Meyers-Briggs Personality Type test and similar tests. You should know where you draw your energy from. Are you an extrovert or an introvert? What if you are a bit of both—an ambivert? I personally find that I need to draw much of my energy internally. I love to read, have as much rest as possible, and thrive from time alone. I'm also very driven and passionate to accomplish personal goals. Others sometimes think I have a chip on my shoulder because I find it difficult to go out and do things without a specific purpose. I know many people who cannot even go to any public functions with lots of people present without being surrounded by even more people! They draw their energy from regular and frequent interactions with people.

People and personality types don't occur in a black-and-white understanding of what they are. Every person can appear on a spectrum of different personality ranges without a diagnosis of some type of disorder. These differences are part of what gives each life the unique potential for adventure and the opportunity to create something the world has never seen before. If we were all the same, none of us would have anything new to contribute to the world around us. Nothing to add. It would be painstakingly predictable. But knowing your inclinations and the intricacies of your personality type can lead to the confidence you need to build the *right* relationships with the right people and set necessary boundaries without isolating yourself from the potential that these beautiful relationships can lead to.

I see relationships as boats. Some are like tug boats that you see less often, and do not need the force to overcome storms and waves, while others are massive – like cruise ships or barges. You stay on these longer, sometimes for months or years. They are built big and strong to withhold the massive impact from the sea. Some boats *do* sink, which is *never* the goal. Try at all costs to never let your boats (relationships) sink! This might happen for many reasons, and sometimes it's beyond our control. We will address this as well.

Why does knowing your personality type matter?

To set this straight, knowing your personality type is not the be-all-end-all when it comes to knowing how to build healthy relationships. But building healthy relationships is *essential*. Sometimes lies can creep in because of previous pain and tell you that you don't need any (or very few) relationships to get where you're going, but I beg to differ. True, you don't *need* many relationships to be successful, but that's almost like saying you don't need many types of food to survive. You might survive on very little, but you might also end up malnourished in areas that you never even knew of until you have your blood-work done. When you notice something alarming in your body, you might not even know how you were malnourished. We need variety, and we are not meant to live in lack in any area of our lives. This includes relationships as well.

Introverts are some of my favorite people. I find them very easy to relate to -

since I am one myself. Let me set the record straight about introverts. An introvert is *not* antisocial, weird, crazy, isolated, unfriendly, or rude. Just the opposite. I find that self-proclaimed introverts are usually aware enough to know where they can safely draw their energy from and how to set appropriate boundaries. An introvert might set such boundaries as "call before you come over my house" or "text me before you call." Often, introverts will need a slight warning to mentally prepare so that they can pour energy and time into a conversation or social interaction. It's not that they don't want to hang out. Introverts might prefer to go rock climbing with friends instead of having a deep conversation over coffee. This might not be true of all introverts, but this might be the case with some types of creative people who are drained from deep connection and bonding. In other instances, introverts actually prefer deep conversation as opposed to surface chit-chat.

Regardless of the case, the person will probably still need some idea of what the interaction will look like ahead of time so they can spend their energy wisely. And this isn't always the case, either, especially with closer relationships. For me personally, I can barely talk on the phone for ten minutes. But even before we were married, I could easily talk on the phone with my husband for several hours at at a time. Even more than that, our interaction energized me, and I found it enjoyable! He was the only person that I could hold these long phone conversations with. Introverts might be shy and sometimes appear more outgoing than they feel, especially if they love people.

I find that extroverts *love* interaction with people. Being surrounded by people really motivates them. Many folks used to believe that to be a true minister, leader, or lover of people, you had to be a strong extrovert. Some have thought over the years that extroverts are healthier mentally and emotionally than introverts. This couldn't be further from the truth! I have found that extroverts have their own struggles. They are often characterized as unreserved or gregarious. If you are a true extrovert, you might find yourself more talkative and energized by social interactions. You might process things externally and be perceived as more friendly than the introvert. These qualities and characteristics are not wrong. You might find that you have to set different boundaries than others.

Realizing who you are, where you draw your energy from, and what relationship types are healthiest for you is important because the right relationships have the potential to elevate you toward your goals and to the right positions of service and leadership.

What is your personality type?

_____

_____

_____

_____

Which do you draw energy from more: Time alone <u>or</u> interaction with others?

_____
_____
_____
_____
_____

What are some boundaries that make your relationships more fruitful so that you aren't exhausted past your limitations?

_____
_____
_____
_____
_____
_____
_____
_____
_____
_____
_____
_____

Chapter 7:

Victim Mentality

Becoming a victim is a result of circumstance, not a permanent identifying factor.

I will address the victim mentality because I want to share some insight on walking in victory. Far too many times, I have seen leaders use their platforms to shame the victim, acting as if he or she brought this mentality upon themselves, or acting as if the person has chosen to be stuck in such a circle of never ending ruts that create a vicious cycle of constantly needing help, ministry, or healing. Although their intention may have been to encourage the people to rise above their circumstances, they may not realize the further damage that was being done.

97

On the other hand, I have also seen people hang on to the smallest obstacles in their lives and use them as excuses to never push past the ongoing issues that tend to distract their focus and derail their success. This, of course is a two fold issue.

Most people have had something bad happen to them. I had to explain this to my two sons the other day. We were studying the Bill of Rights. (Can you tell we homeschool?) The children started asking questions about our right to own a gun in this country. I had to explain many aspects about our freedoms and rights to protect ourselves. They so innocently asked me, "So, Mama, if a person comes in our home and tries to hurt us, do you just kill them dead?"

I responded, "No, loves. Even when someone has bad intentions, we do everything in our power to do as little harm as possible to them while, at the same time, protecting what is ours. And you all are mine, so I will protect you!"

They were slightly shocked, but one

responded, "Yes, and God will protect us because we are His *glory!*"

This is where the hard part comes in. I had to explain to my son right after he had been diagnosed with cancer (at four-and-a-half years old) that terrible things can still happen – even to believers. That is why it's all the *more* important to do our very best each moment, and the Holy Spirit will surely guide us in what to do when we don't naturally know what to do.

That's just the thing. We don't always know what to do or say in every situation, and terrible things can and do happen to some of the most amazing people. I believe that leaders and speakers sometimes think they are helping when they command people to get over their victim mentality. I'm not against the idea that we should rise up, but I believe it is nearly *impossible* for people to truly rise up unless and until they experience empathy and compassion either from a community around them or from God Himself.

Let's Get Shift Done!

If this were an easy topic to address, then therapists, counselors, motivational speakers, mental health workers, case managers, psychiatrists, and the like would all be put out of business. Not only are they not out of business but these kinds of businesses are booming because everyone is searching for reasons and ways to escape what holds them down and holds them back, also known as the "victim mentality." We don't need another sermon on how not to live as victims. We need revelation of how to rise above these things! We need less victim shaming and more leaders walking with the broken on the path to freedom. This is far easier said than done, and I certainly realize that! The only way that the terrible things around us and on the news will improve is when people not only realize they need God, but that they need each other, and they need revelation on their true identity and new nature.

After something bad happens, I believe the first thing that marks a true victim is an attack on their identity. Therein lies the heart of the matter. Once a person is confused about who they are, all their other functions and foundations collapse from underneath them. Take, for example, someone in the human trafficking industry. I have heard reports and watched interviews over and over on the subject to find connections and clues for everything from the motive of the abuser to the tactics and methods he uses to gain control of his victims and then how this brings a formerly healthy person and turns them into a victim.

You see, there is an entire strategy to reprogramming a person to become a victim. Nobody wakes up, hears a sermon on becoming a victim and simply begins to walk as a victim. True victims are targeted and attacked at their core. In one interview, a young woman had been born and bred as a number in the human trafficking industry. She was finally set free in her late twenties. After she made it out of the unbelievable torture she was born into, she had no idea how to function in everyday society. She did not refer to her captor as an evil enemy. She called him the man who owns me. She not only refused to refer to him by any other terms but she continued to use terms in the present tense (owns me) as if she were still his possession.

From birth, her identity was sabotaged. She was told that her parents intended to sell her into the industry upon conception, and she even met her parents who confirmed this. It was one of the saddest stories I had ever heard. Some of the intense abuses she endured included making her act like a dog. This poor woman actually believed that she was *created* for this terrible business, and when she was finally free, she was still bound because she did not know how to walk out her identity of freedom. She was affected by so many years of brainwashing that her victim mentality wasn't going to change because someone told her to rise up and get over it. It would only change through encountering the powerful love of God—the only One at this point who could truly show her why she was *really* created.

She went onto describe how she could tell the people who were born into the slave trade versus the ones who were captured.

She explained that those who were captured fought back. Why would they fight when the ones who were born into it didn't fight? Because the people born into slavery have only ever known a slave identity. The ones who were captured knew they didn't belong there. We can see this same difference in our thought processes when bad things happen to non-believers and believers.

First Thessalonians 4:13 says that we don't "mourn as those who have no hope." This refers directly to death and the hope we carry in eternal life with Jesus. I believe this is the key for believers who suffer from traumatic events. Mourning in and of itself is not a bad thing. But mourning will look differently for those who have hope and those who don't. People who have never really grasped the hope of Jesus will look at a lifestyle of negative events and attribute it to how life is or think "these things always happen to me." Someone with faith and hope will take the time to process through the shock (depending on the situation) and then find hope or encouragement in their faith from their Heavenly Father.

This, of course, does not mean that everyone who proclaims faith in something will have a positive life view. Just because someone goes to church or claims to have faith doesn't mean they have an intimate relationship with God as their Father. Those who are actively living in relationship with their Heavenly Father will be immersed in their heavenly identity.

How to help if you are a leader

Leadership and a passion to help others goes beyond a title or position. It takes more than years of schooling to actually know how to serve. I would propose that the best leadership skills come with experience. I have mentioned before that being a leader or a minister has a very clear, defining objective.

Ministry quite literally means service. Even if you are not in any certain religious position but have picked up this book to learn how to better your own habits and possibly become an even better leader, the key to great leadership is and always will be *service.*

This can be painful at times. Serving is not always easy when the person or people you are serving do not even know what they are hungry for. I was a waitress—quite literally a server—for many years. Some people were so nice and patient and knew exactly what they wanted. Others came in to order something and were extremely ornery and unhappy with any attempt I made to fulfill their requests. This is much like leading. The immediate response you receive from a person you are trying to serve is often not a great gauge of progress. To see true progress in someone's life, you will need to buckle down for the long haul, which can vary for each person. I'd say being a pastor has to be one of the toughest jobs in existence. It takes extreme patience and guidance from the Holy Spirit. This is why you truly should not take up a position in leadership that you are not called to.

Of course, when the person you are trying to serve (or help) presents themselves as a victim, your first response should not be to preach a message from the pulpit on the victim mentality. Even if the timing is appropriate, I still think there are better ways to deal with personal issues aside from preaching about them from the platform. Leading a victim should be a covenant relationship. Depending on how severe the case is, you will need to fulfill different measures of obligation on your part. In some ways, this can become very one-sided.

For the record, it is okay to be in a one-sided position of leadership if you know what you are doing and if you set appropriate boundaries. You can then serve a person with nothing to give but who can only receive in that season. On the contrary, you can also recognize when the problems themselves are over your head and you need to call in more professional services to aid or assist the person in need.

So much of this can be difficult for a new leader to navigate. Sometimes our best efforts to help can lead people into worse situations than they were in to begin with if we do not have the expertise to handle certain serious matters. As a matter of fact, any time someone expresses thoughts of hurting others or themselves, those threats must be promptly reported to the correct legal authorities, according to the law. This is called "mandated reporting" and must be followed.

Boundaries in Leadership

Boundaries seems to be one of the new buzz words of the century. While many great books and resources are available on the subject, you need to define your limits and map out your strategy as to how you will implement these into your leadership.

This is one of my favorite topics because I know that when a person has healthy boundaries, they can make a lasting impact in the world. He or she is taking care of their personal space before allowing others to enter it. It's somewhat like keeping your house clean before you allow guests to enter. Do you have an open door policy at your house? If you do, so many people might be coming in and out of your house that you cannot keep up with the cleaning, the dishes, folding the laundry, and taking care of all the daily tasks related to running a household. Your quality of life suffers in the long run. Do you keep your door locked so that people have to break in to enter? You might have a cleaner house but it will also be a *lonelier* one. You will also only leave room in your life for thieves and robbers since you never open the door for kind-hearted people. The only people you will know will be those who break in and take from you, leading you further into your isolation than when you started.

When you consistently expose yourself to people without appropriate boundaries, this will have a negative effect on your views of others and relationships. If you have a few negative experiences with rejection, you might start to avoid authentic relationships because you fear rejection. This can make you fearful of deepening relationships or make you uncomfortable to be alone for a second if you constantly need to have people around all the time. It can drive you to leave important hallways of your mind and heart unkempt, and you might discover junk in your closets.

When defining your exact boundaries, you have to learn the type of person you are. This is why I mention not only your identity in Christ, but your personality type too. Any book with a narrow-minded approach to boundaries will often have a one-stop-shop attitude toward developing a formula for it. But that's just the thing—no formula works for everyone. Everybody's boundaries will look different.

Sometimes this reality is so drastic that certain people cannot fellowship much together. That's okay! We are all created uniquely, so if you are not called to reach someone through a personal friendship, you will be called to reach someone else. I believe God will lead you to exactly the right people. This is true with leadership as well. When people come into your life, they never become yours. Whether a pastor, evangelist, prophet, apostle, or teacher, I do not believe that people are owned by a certain leadership. While many will not admit this, many ministers view it this way and often refer to their personal congregation as "my people."

I have been in ministry for many years at this point, and I can honestly say whether we were church planting, running schools, helping build someone else's church, or even just working on projects and meetings for our own events, I never looked at people and thought they were "my people" (in a controlling sense of ownership). People who love and are dedicated to the things of God are God's people, no matter whose ministry they are a part of. Leadership is simply stewarding wisdom, revelation, and application in service to God's family, which we are a part of. Many leaders have told me that leadership is simply doing life with people. I agree with many aspects of this, but I also believe it is so much more.

It is supernatural for someone to be carried through life on the joy of the Lord but then to also maintain joy while doing life with people who, many times, look to you for answers they can't seem to find other places.

I once heard a pastor say, "I am a second-generation pastor. That in itself is a miracle!" Ha! How true! I believe my children will be ministers no matter what career path they choose, but we need a true understanding of our fullness to raise children and lead above the politics that often come with being in full-time ministry–to the point where your kids are not jaded but *inspired* to be in ministry themselves. And while it is funny and quite a miracle that a second-generation minister would love ministry himself, it's also our inheritance as believers!

In my previous studies about boundaries, I have found a popular system that includes circles within circles, which I think is great for those of us who are intensely organized. Yet even within these guidelines, we need to take the best parts of these systems and implement them without becoming too rigid so that once we fill up all the available spots in our circles, we stop looking for opportunity to inspire and to be inspired.

In one particular model, Jesus had twelve disciples. Of those twelve, three are closer to him. Beyond those twelve are several outer circles. But as we are drawing our circle maps and figuring out who goes where and why, are we bypassing the entire point? Boundaries exist so that we can dive further into relationships and not box in the ones we already have. I believe that setting your circles too firmly is really binding and isolating yourself to a certain choice group of people. While that's not always the case, I do see this happen. I believe that your relational needs will continue to change in life.

For example, consider a new mother. When the first person in a group of friends becomes pregnant, it can be entirely life-changing for the parents. What happens to that group of friends? Well, they sometimes remain supportive and understanding through all that comes with becoming a parent. Sometimes, however, the get togethers happen less and less often. The new parents usually do not have the same freedoms they did before they had children. Their new interests involve daycares, toddler/mommy groups, or similar activities. The fathers get wrapped up in working even harder for the added expenses that come with raising a family. The parents get less sleep and walk through a new season and all the phases that come with it. This can often lead to finding new friends who are also in a similar season. I believe that your relational needs will sometimes be met from entirely different people in different seasons. As you take care of your relational needs, you might also be fulfilling someone else's needs as well!

I've heard it said that everything you will ever need comes out of relationships— first, our relationship with God and then our relationship with everyone else. If we are too careful, too limiting, and too concerned with putting everyone into their proper circle in our relationship diagrams, we might miss the very people who should be introduced into our lives for the next season that we haven't even seen coming.

This is also why it's important to appreciate people in general. I once knew someone who claimed to love God but hated people. You can't do this. You can say that you do, but you can't thrive in this type of thinking over the long-term. You will need to choose one or the other. Opening your heart to God means you will open your heart to people. Closing your heart to people means you will close your heart to God. There's no way around that, so you will need to navigate these situations with guidance from the Holy Spirit. If you feel hatred toward people, seek help as soon as possible so that you don't sabotage your whole life with unnecessary heartache.

Reflect on some of the experiences you have had as a victim. How did you overcome that mentality? Does this perspective still affect you today? How has that shaped your reality? How might you use it to help someone else through your vulnerability?

_____

_____

_____

_____

_____

_____

_____

_____

_____

_____

_____

_____

_____

_____

_____

_____

What healthy boundaries do you feel have helped you maintain your relationships? What, if any, could you improve on to be open to new relationships in your life?

_____

_____

_____

_____

_____

_____

_____

_____

_____

_____

_____

Chapter 8:

The best, most effective way to introduce the heart of God to someone who is hurting is simply to *become* God's heart for that person. My husband, Rob, an international writer and speaker, will often open up his messages with a pair of glasses that either say Jesus on them or that actually have a picture of Jesus on them. He does this to make people wonder why he is wearing those goofy glasses. Then he gets to speak into people about seeing others through Jesus lenses. This has been such a powerful and impactful tool over the years.

In order to gain the insight needed to help people see God's heart for them, first look at the person with God's heart. Interestingly enough, when I became a mother, whenever I saw babies around town or out and about, I no longer saw them as other people's children. I saw them through a mother's eyes with a mother's perspective. I saw any child as my own child with the same heart to love, grow, and protect them. As my children grew, and as I became older, I even started to do this with teens. I eventually learned to see people my age and older as somebody's children. Over time, I started to see them with the heart of a mother—the heart of a parent. I asked God, "What is this about? I can see people three times the age of my child. I care for them. I want to help them. I want to serve them." I felt as if God was showing me his heart for people, his heart for His children. I have this "Jesus vision" so intensely now that at any moment, I no longer see people in a grocery store just walking about. I no longer see people on the street. I see children. Children everywhere. They are God's children, and because He's put such a love in my heart for humanity, they are my children to serve and care for as well. It's an incredible feeling to love humanity and have the privilege to see people the way He does.

I'd like to clarify as I stated before that I do not see people as "my people"–meaning that I own them and make decisions for them. But just as I raise my children with the intention of loving and serving them, I desire to come alongside them and help them reach their full potential. I want to hear their dreams and their desires. I want to walk with them through the hardships and celebrate the victories, and *this* is the true heart of the Father for His people: Humanity! That's who Jesus *died* for! He didn't die for believers! He died for the world!

Let that sink in for a minute.

He didn't die for believers . . . *He died for the **world!***

And those are the people we are called to serve. Not just the local church. Not just the food pantry. What about the homeless in the street? What about the drug abusers in prison? What about the married men hiding their wedding rings at bars? Those—and others like them—are the people we are called to serve alongside believers!

When God brings a special case into your life, you can be his heart. He will not leave you wondering how to do it. He will lead and guide you through the situation.

You cannot be taught intimacy; it must be displayed through example.

One of the most impacting yet forgotten values of our culture is intimacy. How many people do we hear preaching about the lost art of connection and intimacy due to the technological age we are in today? In some ways, they are absolutely right. Why have we lost the art of authenticity in relationships?

When I was growing up, your parents' separation or divorce was almost as much of a milestone in a young person's life as getting their driver's license. Today, it's a common story that most people share. The way everyone deals with a situation like this can vary greatly and while for some, it has seemingly little if any impact, it throws others into a tail spin. Regardless, I can say that the most damaging of effects with an epidemic of this magnitude is that we have lost most of our heroes who could model what intimacy really is. Families have become so broken over the generations. These problems have always existed, but maybe now, it's just more magnified because news is so widespread that we are more aware of our issues than ever. Nevertheless our generation is in a crisis. We are begging for intimacy and don't know where to find it. Worse than that, the mothers and fathers we look to don't know where to find it either!

This isn't an unsolvable crisis even for those in our generation who have been through terrible family or relationship breakups. The only way we will resurrect intimacy in our generation, however, is by first experiencing intimacy with God.

What does it mean to have intimacy with God? The definition of intimacy itself is a *"close familiarity or friendship; closeness."* (Source: Google Dictionary)

Scripture tells us that we are to have an intimate relationship with God. Psalm 25:14 (AMP) declares, *"The secret [of the sweet, satisfying companionship] of the Lord have they who fear (revere and worship) Him, and He will show them His covenant and reveal to them its [deep, inner] meaning."*

In Amos 3:7 (KJV), Amos also teaches that the Lord reveals his secrets to the prophets. *"Surely the Lord God will do nothing, but he revealeth his secret unto His servants the prophets."*

In one of my favorite scriptures regarding the topic of intimacy, Jesus even equates what He accomplished at the cross, stating that a man "gives his life for his friends." *"Greater love has no one than this, than to lay down one's life for his friends" (John 15:13 NIV).*

These scriptures clearly display God's heart for intimacy with His people. We often find that to take the first step in the direction of intimacy requires vulnerability and the person desiring intimacy will often have to take a step of faith by putting forth their own vulnerability first. This is exactly what God did with humanity. He took a chance. He put His heart into His creation. He made friendships with humanity, and in doing so, He put His heart on a platter by trusting them with His secrets. Do you think God didn't know our capacity for betrayal? He certainly does, but Jesus didn't let that stop Him from demonstrating His love for us anyway!

"Faithful are the wounds of a friend, but the kisses of an enemy are deceitful" (Proverbs 27:6 KJV).

More likely than not, someone you consider a friend will end up hurting you—or even worse, betraying you—at some point. Even with this knowledge, God wanted to have friendship with His people. He then goes onto describe how humanity can reciprocate that same intimacy.

"You are my friends if you do whatever I command you" (John 15:14 ESV).

What a powerful thought! We have access to friendship, closeness, and intimacy with the living God of all creation! Wow! You might feel overwhelmed at the thought of doing what God commands you, or perhaps your mind goes to every Bible verse with a "command" in it. If so, be at ease and learn a simple short cut to following all the laws today:

"Teacher, which is the greatest commandment in the Law?" (Matthew 22:36 NIV).

"Jesus replied, 'Love the Lord your God with all your heart and with all your soul and with all your mind. This is the first and greatest commandment. And the second is like it: Love your neighbor as yourself.' All the Law and the Prophets hang on these two commandments."

If your heart and actions can be renewed to the point where everything that flows out of you is love for God with all your heart, soul, and mind and love for other people (your neighbors), then every other command or law given will be fulfilled by just focusing on these two. Every possible commandment given in scripture is fulfilled in those two.

You might ask, "Well, what about the commandments to not steal or to not bear false witness?"

If you truly love God and others as He commands us to do, you naturally won't steal or lie about or to them.

It's quite simple, and we overcomplicate these matters. We become friends with God when we follow His commands. When we follow His commands, we will simply abide in the fruit of the Spirit: love! If we are abiding in love, everything else that flows from us will be good and will reflect friendship with God. We will even notice the supernatural world around us more. We will start to have incredible, detailed prophetic dreams and visions because God will start to share His secrets with us. We will know things that we couldn't have known without his insight. We will be able to exhort and encourage people we haven't even met before, but we will receive a word for them in that moment.

You see, even if the rug has been ripped out from under your feet in the area of intimacy—from parents or a failed relationship or church hurt or business betrayal or past relationships with others—we can still learn intimacy with God. His heart is right there. He is ready to share in this deep relationship with you. And once you open up to this kind of relationship with God, you will start to be able to show intimacy in your relationships with others.

Summary:

What is your current view of intimacy? Has this view been previously damaged by a relationship that turned sour that was supposed to model this kind of closeness in your life?

_____
_____
_____
_____
_____
_____
_____
_____

Meditate on the scriptures in this chapter regarding friendship with God. Ask God for that intimacy in your relationship with him. Ask him to share his secrets with you. Ask and thank him for a heart for people. Document what he shares with you:

_____

_____

_____

_____

_____

_____

_____

_____

_____

_____

_____

_____

_____

_____

_____

_____

Chapter 9: Character

I've shared some key details of my journey: a positive mindset, the difference between confidence and pride, understanding humility versus timidity, relationships, knowing your identity and your personality type, boundaries, overcoming a victim mentality, the path to victory, leadership, and more. But I've decided to save some of the best chapters for last!

Out of everything I've shared thus far, character is the tool that is the foundation of it all! You can have all the best formulas, protocols, and gimmicky memory slogans to know exactly how you should be performing as a believer and a leader, but character is what will actually reach into the depths of who you are and transform your life. Character is what will maintain all those other efforts over the long-term. One of the most valuable reasons that character is so important is because it's the evidence of your belief in God. You simply cannot accept the good news of what Jesus has done for you and in you and have your character remain the same as before. You cannot possibly function with a poor character when you know the truth about your destiny.

"A tree is identified by its fruit. If a tree is good, its fruit will be good. If a tree is bad, its fruit will be bad" (Matthew 12:33 NLT).

"Does a spring of water bubble out with both fresh water and bitter water? Does a fig tree produce olives, or a grapevine produce figs? No, and you can't draw fresh water from a salty spring"(James 3:11–12 NLT).

Does this mean we need to fix the water if salty water comes out of a spring? Are we going to pick out every grain of salt from the water? No! We would need an entirely new well.

And what about that tree that produces bad fruit? Should we do some kind of healing project or fruit restoration project? Not so! But this is what so much of the church does today. (I'm not church bashing. I absolutely *love* the church and could not live without being part of one myself, but I am referring here to the church as a body. Church traditions have been carried out in false teachings and doctrines, leading many to believe they can control fruit by managing the behavior of others instead of encouraging people to walk in an entirely new mindset.)

If the tree is producing the bad fruit, the tree is bad. Period. Cut that sucker down! Yes, you heard me right! Throw it away! Should we throw ourselves away if we are continually producing bad fruit? Guess what —you don't have to. Why not? Because you are functioning from a nature that's already dead. You will not be able to bear long-lasting, good fruit from that bad mindset because that bad sinful mindset is dead. It's like jumping into a dead car with no engine. This vehicle has no possibility of going anywhere because the engine is completely gone. It looks as if it has a functioning body, but it won't go anywhere unless some outside force pushes and moves it. It has not power and is a dead work in itself.

If you put that dead, engineless vehicle on top of a hill and get into it, you can push it downhill with all your might. Once that vehicle starts moving, there's no way to stop it. It's destined to crash and burn.

Your old, dead mindset works the same way. You can't function from that place any longer. And although we talked about positivity, this is slightly different. This is more than just a perception change or a different viewpoint. This is a reality change. The reality of sin is dead to you now. Once you become a believer in what Jesus has done in you, you are no longer a sinner saved by grace. You are no longer a sinner at all! You are now *grace*! Your whole being and existence is "Christ in you, the hope of glory!

"I have been crucified with Christ and I no longer live, but Christ lives in me. The life I now live in the body, I live by faith in the Son of God, who loved me and gave himself for me" (Galatians 2:20 NIV).

You are not some dirty person who has to clean up your behavior. If your behavior is inconsistent with the reality of a saint of the most holy God, then you need to really believe the good news of Jesus. You need to accept that crucifixion with Jesus deep into your belief system, not because your acceptance of it makes it true but because that truth is the *only* thing with the power to transform your being from the inside out so that you line up with your destiny from the foundation of the world.

Now I know that was a *huge* glory bomb to drop all in one chapter, and books upon books have been written on this topic that go into much more depth that what I did. But this is the most important chapter in this book. Let your fruit be a reality of what you truly believe! If your fruit isn't bearing that out, you might need to ask yourself some key questions. You may want to pray a prayer similar to the following, which I call *"The Saint's Prayer"*:

"Jesus, I thank you for the work you did on the cross and that you forgave my sins two thousand years ago. I believe that I have been crucified with you, and my sin nature was nailed to that very same cross. I believe I am now a *new creation*, and I choose to function from my renewed mindset as many times as I have to renew it with the truth that I am your child! I produce good fruit. I can share this good news with others because it fills me with joy. I am no longer under condemnation, and my conviction is joy!"

This is just such a small sample of what you might really pray, say, think, or believe, but it's a great starting point, especially if you've never heard a message quite like this before.

This is the entirety of how your character will be built. In effect, your character is your belief system. It's truth in action behind the scenes and on the platform. It will reveal everything about who you are.

Character (n) - the aggregate of features and traits that form the individual nature of some person or thing. (www.dictionary.com/browse/character)

Character

Character is so profoundly deep inside a person that it's the aggregate or collection of features and traits that form the nature or essence of a person. This is why character can only be formed or fixed through your belief system. I'm not sure that I've ever heard of any so-called self-help program that has actually cured or even changed a person's character.

The only thing I've truly seen change a person's character to the core of who they are is the gospel of Jesus Christ. That is why it's essential to start there when any problematic issues arise in a person's life.

This is not to say that other programs can't help. I have known many victims of terrible things in this world, and people really struggle when they have to navigate through these difficulties on their own. They can process trauma much more smoothly in therapy and in similar programs. It can be essential to have counsel and accountability when going through intense personal healing, but these forms of accountability should bring you back to your renewed identity and not allow you to fall into your old nature, whether it be sin or negativity or even just remaining emotionally or mentally handicapped under the guise of lies you are tempted to believe. I understand that this is rarely easy, but if one form of therapy or program isn't working for you, look for another. You might need to try different options because sometimes it's difficult to find someone who really believes in renewing the mind as a new creation.

Summary:

Does the fruit of my life line up with what I believe? If not, what are some areas I might need to renew my mind in regarding my character?

_____

_____

_____

_____

_____

_____

_____

Have you relied on therapies or programs that use techniques and formulas that do not lead you to believe and function with your renewed mind? How might you incorporate thinking with your renewed mind into these techniques and formulas?

_____
_____
_____
_____
_____
_____
_____
_____
_____
_____
_____
_____
_____
_____
_____

Chapter 10: Be Resourceful
(Act Within Your Resources)

As a child in school, my teachers told me that I could be *anything* I wanted to be. While I understand the concept they wanted us to grasp, this is not entirely true. Anyone cannot become anything they want to be. We are, however, all given enough resources to make the most of what we have. Most people never learn how to make the most of their resources or how to turn their resources into seed so that their resources serve as assets to them and their dreams. Instead they say that the rich become richer and the poor become poorer. Why is that? I believe it comes down to this:

Mindset

In Luke 8, Jesus tells the parable of the sower.

"One day Jesus told a story in the form of a parable to a large crowd that had gathered from many towns to hear him: "A farmer went out to plant his seed. As he scattered it across his field, some seed fell on a footpath, where it was stepped on, and the birds ate it. Other seed fell among rocks. It began to grow, but the plant soon wilted and died for lack of moisture. Other seed fell among thorns that grew up with it and choked out the tender plants. Still other seed fell on fertile soil. This seed grew and produced a crop that was a hundred times as much as had been planted!"" (Luke 8:4–8 NLT).

Throughout this passage, Jesus specifically refers to the seed as the gospel. But I see something else hidden in this message.

Jesus uses something we can see and parallel this to life in order to make his message clear. He uses resources to show us exactly how he is establishing His covenant and kingdom with His people. He describes the different kinds of resources each seed has to its advantage or disadvantage based on where it is planted.

Where you are planted and what you have available to you has everything to do with making the most of what you have. That sounds almost backwards, but you can see this in the most practical sense. In order to truly be resourceful, you need to see your current resources as potential assets or as seeds.

The seeds thrown on the rocks, thorns, and gravel don't have much to work with. The sower seemed to be completely careless and unintentional when he sowed his seeds, or he might have harvested so much more. That's a sad story considering that the verse says he *intentionally* went out to sow his seeds.

You can also read a similar story in Matthew 25, the parable of the talents. This story, in fact, goes into even greater detail with examples.

"For it is just like a man going on a journey, who called his servants and entrusted them with his possessions. To one he gave five talents, to another two talents, and to another one talent—each according to his own ability. And he promptly went on his journey.

The servant who had received five talents went and put them to work, and gained five more. Likewise, the one with two talents gained two more. But the servant who had received one talent went off, dug a hole in the ground, and hid his master's money.

After a long time, the master of those servants returned to settle accounts with them. The servant who had received five talents came and presented five more. 'Master,' he said, 'you entrusted me with five talents. See, I have gained five more.'

His master replied, 'Well done, good and faithful servant! You have been faithful with a few things; I will put you in charge of many things. Enter into the joy of your master!'

Then the servant who had received two talents also came and said, 'Master, you entrusted me with two talents. See, I have gained two more.'

His master replied, 'Well done, good and faithful servant! You have been faithful with a few things; I will put you in charge of many things. Enter into the joy of your master!'

Finally, the servant who had received one talent came and said, 'Master, I knew that you are a hard man, reaping where you have not sown, and gathering where you have not scattered seed. So in my fear, I went and hid your talent in the ground. See, you have what belongs to you.'

'You wicked, lazy servant!' replied his master. 'You knew that I reap where I have not sown and gather where I have not scattered seed. Then you should have deposited my money with the bankers, and on my return I would have received it back with interest.

Therefore take the talent from him and give it to the one who has ten talents. For everyone who has will be given more, and he will have an abundance. But the one who does not have, even what he has will be taken away from him." (Matthew 25:14–29, BSB).

The parable addresses how each person with his different mindsets takes the money given to them and either creates growth with it or does nothing at all. What stands out most, I believe, is the verse that says, "For everyone who has will be given more, and he will have an abundance. But the one who does not have, even what he has will be taken away from him." I do not believe that God is looking for opportunities to take from us. I believe this is a wake-up call to think about our mindsets and the resources we have available to us. Those who have will see what they have as seed and will invest into greater resources with their current resources. Those who don't have will try to hold onto what they have in fear of being without. In turn, they will end up without.

This is a poverty mindset, and I struggled with it for years. Boy, was it ever a step of faith to walk across the border from Texas to Central and South America with my

144

husband, knowing we would trek through all twenty-one nations by land with only a thousand dollars to our name. (The money had just been given to us by our partners who saw us to our last flight on the way to the journey.) If you have any sense about finances, you will realize that a thousand dollars is not nearly enough to last for nine months while traveling through twenty-one nations. But God! And here we are today. That journey taught me so much about letting go of a poverty mindset and seeing resources as seed. So much of living by faith is doing exactly that.

Many people believe that living by faith means living without resources, but living by faith actually means that you see the resources you are given as seed. You see your seed turn into assets and then see those assets as more seed.

Each of the servants were given different resources with different abilities and could then expand those resources. Whether or not they expanded those resources was not dependent on how much they had nor was it dependent on their ability to do more with it. It was solely dependent on their mindset for growth or their fear of lack.

I grew up in a home with very little, and I used to be fearful of getting rid of things. I kept old stale chips in my cupboards as a grown woman in case something happened and we suddenly needed food. I obsessed over the times as a child when I didn't have food and thought if I got rid of things—no matter what that was—I would end up in lack.

You know the joke when a mother looks in the refrigerator and finds a carton of milk with just a swallow of milk left at the bottom? Well, that was me! I believed, "There's still a little bit in there!" I couldn't bear the idea of being without. And while, of course, I don't believe we should purposefully waste resources, I was functioning in a fear of lack. This very mindset stands in the way of just getting your shoes on, going to the store, and buying more. Instead of holding onto those old habits, you can get off the couch and do something about it!

When you feel as if you have a call to do something on this earth, be resourceful. Work within your resources and influence. You can, of course, dream by faith but also act within the reality of your faith too. God might have planted real life resources in your grasp so that you can take those as seeds for the greater things you feel He is calling you to!

Right now, think about some of the biggest dreams God has put in your heart. Write down one of those dreams below. Next think about the resources—the possible seeds and assets—you have available to you. How might you be able to grow in the direction of those God-given dreams with the resources you already have?

_____

_____

_____

_____

_____

_____

_____

_____

_____

_____

_____

_____

_____

_____

_____

_____

_____

_____

Chapter 11:

Self Control (The Sound Mind)

You are *never* too old and *never* too young! I wanted to include some encouragement in the direction of age as that is one of the main things that people let stand in the way of their dreams. The young ones are too focused on the pressure to build a life and the older ones feel defeated by the belief that it's too late. It's not too early, and it's not too late to have an impact when it comes to your dreams! It's not too early or late to look at the resources around you and plant seed for future generations. It's not too late to change your mindset and your viewpoint and begin to live a positive life that impacts those around you. I could pull out many examples of this from the Bible and from history. Scholars believe that Mary was about fourteen years old when she birthed Jesus. Josiah became king when he was just seven years old. (See 2 Kings 11:21.) Abraham and Sarah inherited the promise of birthing nations at 100 and 90, respectively, an age we would be uncomfortable thinking about children. There's no excuse or reason why your life can't be completely different tomorrow than it is today. Whatever the case, if these thoughts are defeating you, surround yourself with *doers*—others who are walking out their vision. These trapping thoughts regarding limitations and fear of lack are birthed in isolation and designed to keep you there.

As much as I wish that I didn't have to bring this up, I need to mention it. Too many people are torn down by not only their own unbelief in their own God-given potential. At the same time, they are combatting gossip, lies and fits of jealousy from others. This is probably one of the hardest sections of this book for me to write, not because I haven't experienced it, because I have. Not because I haven't forgiven, because I have also done that. It's hard to touch on this subject because I believe it is one of the most destructive tools in action against people today. If the enemy can't take a body out as a whole and all at once, he will start with a little infection that, if it isn't treated, will end up killing the entire body. The smallest forms of unforgiven betrayal can isolate you so badly that you question everything about life in general. It might only take one small instance of gossip, betrayal, backstabbing, or the like to isolate you. In that case, the assignment has come full circle. The temptation to give up in those moments is pivotal. It might take years of saying you forgive the people before you can actually pray for them, but until you can pray for them, you haven't fully forgiven them. And until you can fully forgive them, you will always be hiding behind some form of isolation: never leaving your house or avoiding people at the store or changing churches or other coping methods. Your focus won't be on what you are called to do to change the world around you for the better; it will be on self-preservation in the presence of your enemies. These are key things to work through so that they don't hold you back from the amazing destiny that God has for you!

You might have to work through forgiveness for your whole life, which might mean a whole lot of praying for people who have or who do hurt you. You will also need to remain in intentional communion with God. Yes, he is in us, but we need to focus on our relationship with him and with people and be intentional about our relationship with them as well. People sometimes say, "I love God, just not his people." This might sound cliché or cool, but it's simply not the truth. You cannot "hate your brother and say you love God."

"Whoever claims to love God yet hates a brother or sister is a liar. For whoever does not love their brother and sister, whom they have seen, cannot love God, whom they have not seen" (1 John 4:20, NIV).

In time, on this journey, you will find that the more you see through the eyes of the Father, the more love you will have for people and even those who hurt you. Just when this starts to seem like an elementary concept, something might happen so that you have to put this into practice in your life, so don't forget this point. Never stop loving people and maintain such a renewed mind that you see people how he sees them and not how you do in your circumstances.

But is control all bad?

The first thing a person usually does when hearing the word 'control' is shudder. We have all experienced it in some form or another, and it is all the more painful when it stemmed from a relationship of trust or during a time when we were trying to heal, further plummeting us into despair. Control is something that we as believers are *supposed* to do. Before you yell at me in frustration and quit reading, hear me out. We are not at all intended to control each other. Too many people don't understand this. Sometimes pastors or ministers think it's their job to protect the sheep. I saw this quote a while back on social media that said, "He says to feed my sheep, not fix my sheep. If we feed the sheep, the fixing will happen in the food!"

I couldn't have said that better myself! If we are doing the right things as leaders—setting appropriate boundaries and believing in people the way we should—we will never need to control them. This takes a mindset of victory over fear. You need to be over the fear of losing your ministry or church, and you need to truly have faith and trust that in your decision-making, you will not control anyone. When you are in that mindset, you will not only overcome the fear of losing your church or ministry, but instead your ministry or church will expand. When people feel free to be who they are as part of the platform God has given you, they will be open to the counsel you have to give, and they will want to sow into your vision.

Oh, how ministries would explode if they would just learn that people do not need or want to be controlled. The ones who think they do need healing because once control enters the picture, the situation becomes worse for them and the controlling participant.

While we should not control others and they should not control us, we are still meant to control. "What in the world do you mean by that, Millie?"

One of the fruits of the Spirit listed in Galatians 5:22 is self-control. You see, for many years, I thought I had mastered the concept of "submission" as a wife. I was indecisive and tip-toed around everything and everyone. I thought that not having an opinion made me a more submissive person. I often felt lost and alone and did not know what I was supposed to do in all my life roles. Don't get me wrong, I was surrounded by a husband and people who loved me, but in my own head, striving to remain without an opinion left me feeling suffocated. We weren't meant to live as robots, void of thoughts and ideas and opinions, and so many times, many women in the Christian faith are told that's how they should live.

It took me quite a while to seek out what was not clicking in my life so that being a mother and wife would become more natural. Moms often come to me and ask how I accomplish all that I do from writing to speaking, to homeschooling and finishing Bible college while regularly working out twice a day.

155

As maturity set in after one, two, three children and more (I have five as of the writing of this book), I learned the joy of control—not controlling my circumstances or my family or those around me, but controlling myself.

As I mentioned before, my personality and background included growing up in the northeast United States. A strong work ethic and education are integral parts of the culture, and these were ingrained in me. These ideas didn't only stem from my mother but from school teachers and other adults I came into contact with. This was simply the culture.

Even so, working hard was never an issue for me. Learning to exercise self-control meant so much more than working hard because it meant controlling who I was and controlling my actions without controlling the complete outcome or circumstances surrounding my choices. Self-control meant having my own likes and desires and learning when to slow down and take ownership of my rest also. It meant looking at my babies and saying, "These are my babies, and I have enough self-control to be a good mother to them! I can do whatever it takes to raise them well." And it meant having that same courage even when my husband was on week-long trips to the other side of the world.

If we learned what a blessing control can be and if we learned how to effectively control ourselves, we would never need to control another person again. We would be free to work hard and rest hard. We would not fear of failure, and we would try new things. We would take on big ventures that look supernatural to the human eye because many times, they are. I believe parenting is a very supernatural undertaking. Some people will never be satisfied or have the courage to parent to even their own standards until they know who they are in Christ. This can be applied to many other things, especially in the business world, but I am focusing on parenting right now as that is so much of my world.

Being without opinions and dull doesn't make you more submissive. It takes true courage to release who you really are and to learn to access control over that person and that person alone.

Summary:

Are there areas you need to forgive because someone tried to unjustly control you?

_____
_____
_____
_____
_____
_____
_____
_____
_____

What are some practical steps you can take toward controlling yourself and your choices without needing to control the outcome of your decisions?

_____
_____
_____
_____
_____

Self Control

_____
_____
_____
_____
_____
_____
_____
_____
_____
_____
_____
_____
_____
_____
_____
_____
_____
_____
_____
_____
_____
_____
_____
_____
_____
_____
_____

Chapter 12: The Unique You

So many want to define identity as our culture, our nature, or as a new creation from a Christian perspective. They are not the same thing. Our nature makes up all of what we are in cohabitation and existence with our brothers and sisters to our left and our right. It makes up one body of believers.

You possess certain qualities and traits that nobody else can offer the world. If no two snowflakes are exactly alike, how much more would God have designed each human being as different and unique? There are things about you, I believe, that you have yet to discover. Why do I believe this? How would I know this about you? I believe this because I think we are always discovering and developing our giftings in more intricate ways all the time as long as we are looking for ways to develop them!

You see, you do not have to be anybody's doppelganger! As I write this book, my husband has also just released incredibly powerful book that I believe will change the world and how we think culturally. I believe it will cause a paradigm shift in people's theologies. I'm just now learning concepts that he has known for years and years! As much as I've heard him preach, teach, and release revelation, I still cannot wait to get my hands on his book!

But if you were to compare my book with his, you would see that they are two completely different works of art. I believe my book will also have a profound impact on the world, which is why I spent so much time pouring my heart into it.

For a two-week season, however, I put the book aside to take a break. I was as passionate about it as ever, and whenever I went to proofread or edit a section, the whole purpose for this book was validated. (This might sound strange to write about a book that you are currently writing, but it is the truth!) I'm in a season of intense study about, of all things, theology, which I'm not naturally inclined to understand. With the support of my husband, it has been such a revelatory season for me. Even so, I struggled to find value in what I was pouring out.

I started to wonder about the importance of helping people motivate themselves to pursue a shift in their lives, discover truth about their new nature, and dig deep into their identity. I really wasn't even sure if what I had to offer had any value unless I could derive some deep, new theological revelation that nobody has ever thought of. If I couldn't do that, perhaps my book was useless.

Around the time that these emotions swirled inside me, I began to study emotional intelligence and its importance. I believe that the impact someone can have by strengthening their emotional intelligence is far greater than what they can have by increasing their intellectual intelligence (IQ).

Did you know that if IQ were all that mattered, everyone with a high IQ would most likely be rich and famous? But they are not. Understanding how your actions affect those around you can make all the difference in your success.

Knowing your identity and having a high emotional intelligence can make all the difference in your life, your ministry, and the lives of those you wish to impact.

I've met some of the most incredible, intelligent, and profound teachers from around the world. Some have told us stories of times they have ruined relationships with people because they were immature or were labeled a certain way because of their past decisions. These ruined relationships were not even necessarily because of their message, their appearance, denomination, or anything of the sort.

Some of their biggest issues in business or ministry were issues with knowing when and how to exercise emotional intelligence.

The point of this book is not emotional intelligence. But the more you have of it, the greater and the more fearlessly you can approach the shift in your life. The more humbly you can embrace your mistakes and learn from them. The more you can accept who you truly are and make the most of your resources. The more you can train your mind to focus on heavenly things, on hope, and change your words from negative to confidence and positive. The more you can function from fruit and productivity. The point of this book is to do what only you can do for you. It's to get up, stop feeling sorry for yourself, and make *shift* happen, even when it hasn't naturally happened yet!

As I realized the purpose and impact this book has the potential of making, I learned something about myself as the writer. I learned my identity. I might end up writing a book in the future about theology. For now, however, that's not what flows out of me.

I'm an encourager, author, minister, public speaker, and mother of four with one on the way. I've overcome insurmountable odds, including walking out of mental health institutions and abuse. I'm homeschooling four children when I slept through high school classes and dropped out of college. I fell in love with health and fitness after being classified as morbidly obese. I held my son down through painful chemotherapy treatments and prayed for God to give me the cancer my little four-year-old boy had to endure and to take it from him. I traveled the world with only a couple of dollars in my pocket. I was most definitely *"not* supposed" to make it in this world. I learned that if shift doesn't just happen for me, then I can rise up and *make shift happen*!

You see, your gifts and callings might not look like everyone else's. They might not look like anyone else's. But your gifts and callings are no less important on any scale. This journey of life is an adventure ride to discover who you are. Each time you learn something new about yourself, you discover something about your identity. It's as if you are unwrapping a gift the Father gave directly to you. The fact that it looks different means it's unique. Not only that, but it shows that the Father communicates and designs us personally. How much more special can you feel than that? People sometimes joke about feeling special. It seems as if we shouldn't care about being special once we reach a certain level of maturity.

I say that in jest because I truly believe that as we journey in maturity, we embrace our unique individuality. We understand how special we are to the kingdom of heaven.

And in knowing and embracing these newfound truths, we can embark on even greater adventures for our lives and achieve way beyond what we have ever dreamed before!

There are no boundaries, no limitations outside of what you believe is impossible or outside your resources. You might think, "I don't have a lot of resources," but I can promise you that even with the most limited resources, you can still achieve great things.

A man from a third-world country sent emails to people, requesting money. This is a common story, and we've likely heard dozens like it. People in some third-world nations have very limited resources, leading to intense desperation.

Sometimes these people from Africa steal the identities of people from first-world nations and then acquire large sums of money from people's bank accounts. Well, this seemed like that type of case. The recipient of this email wasn't going to stand for it, but he had a feeling that he should look into the situation. This man from Africa wasn't actually trying to scam him. He wasn't asking for much either but wanted help or ideas on how to feed his community. Together they thought up a plan. The first-world businessman sent a camera to the man in Africa. He had a knowledge of photography and instructed the man to take pictures with tips and pointers on getting the best results. The man did just as he said and sent the camera back to America. The American man was then able to make the photos public, displaying the need and the beauty of Africa.

He decided to auction off these pictures and send the money to Africa to help the community. The man from Africa was not another con artist as most first-world Americans might have thought at first. Together the two men came up with creative resources to provide an answer to the desperate need.

Some of us have so many resources and hang our heads with no ideas as to how to make an impact in the world or how to make our dreams come true. Nonsense! I realize we all have seasons of struggle, but vision is birthed first in your heart, strategy in your head, and action from your passion. You need to allow yourself to dream big and really look at the resources you have! You can do *so* incredibly much with so little.

Chapter 13: Rest

Out of everything I have shared with you, I will leave you with one of the most difficult concepts for myself and many others to fully grasp and put into practice.

One of the most foundational scriptures of the Christian faith is Matthew 11:28–30 NIV. *"Come to me, all you who are weary and burdened and I will give you rest. Take my yoke upon you and learn from me, for I am gentle and humble in heart, and you will find rest for your souls. For my yoke is easy and my burden is light."*

Living in rest is probably the most powerful and strategic tool God gave us to overcome how crazy life can sometimes be.

I am known for ministering to people who struggle with all sorts of mental illnesses. I am not limited to that, but I attract many who suffer from that because they see that I have attained freedom and they want to see that same freedom manifest in their own lives. I've noticed, however, when people contact me with these intense struggles, they are struggling at night more than 90 percent of the time. Why is this? Are people only susceptible to these kinds of issues at night? No, but these thoughts happen when we should be resting and sleeping. Many times, people do not notice. They will explain to me all that is happening in their lives, and they do not realize that they are exhausted. As if going through these struggles wasn't enough, they were up all night worrying about their problems, and just like that, they feel defeated.

Sometimes the best advice I have for people is this. "I will pray for you, but you are tired. So let's pray, and you go to sleep, and we can tackle a new strategy tomorrow.

If life is hard, and you really need to overcome some difficulties, the enemy's best strategy is to attack your sleep and your rest.

Mark 4:35–38 NIV says, *"That day when evening came, he said to his disciples, 'Let us go over to the other side.' Leaving the crowd behind, they took him along, just as he was, in the boat. There were also other boats with him. A furious squall came up, and the waves broke over the boat, so that it was nearly swamped. Jesus was in the stern, sleeping on a cushion. The disciples woke hi and said to him, "Teacher, don't you care if we drown?"*

Let's go over verse 37 and 38 quickly. A huge squall, (a sudden violent gust of wind or localized storm according to the New Oxford American Dictionary Online - https://en.oxforddictionaries.com/definition/sq uall) came up—so huge that the waves were coming over the boat!

The disciples panicked. But where was Jesus during this mess? Where was their hero in the midst of this great tragedy possibly waiting to happen?

Oh, yes. He was sleeping in the boat

As everyone else is frantically wondering what to do, Jesus is sleeping.

As a bit of a Type A personality, I can imagine their frustration.

Jesus is resting peacefully, and the disciples shout and wake him up. "Don't you even care if we drown? Was this your big plan for saving the world?"

Jesus is rest manifested. He is perfect peace in the storm. When life seems to be falling apart all around you, Jesus hands you a cushion and says, "Come, let's take a nap together."

This is not to imply that we have no active role to play in the kingdom. This is simply to say that when you place your heart at peace in Jesus, you will rest in knowing that his authority over your storm takes precedence over the storm itself.

"He got up, rebuked the wind and said to the waves, "Quiet! Be still!" Then the wind died down and it was completely calm. He

*said to his disciples, "Why are you so afraid?
Do you still have no faith?" Mark 4:39–40
NIV*

Take notice of how Jesus equates the
disciple's restlessness with their lack of faith.
The most evident fruit of faith is rest. You can
do all things in your power to make the storm
calm, but Jesus had already been training the
disciples in ministry and trusted that they
would be activated in the authority he gave
them, which is probably why he was resting
so soundly. He thought, "These are my
disciples. I've taught them well. They've got
this covered." He was surprised when they
woke him in terror of the storm, so much so
that he rebuked them.

"Come on, guys, are we back at square
one? Do you still have no faith? I gave you
guys these answers!" And he proceeds to
handle the storm himself.

How you rest is evidence of your faith.

The Bible gives many examples of

God's rest and how it applies to us. One of my favorites is Hebrews 4:8–11 ESV.

"For if Joshua had given them rest, God would not have spoken of another day later on. So then, there remains a Sabbath rest for the people of God, for whoever has entered God's rest has also rested from his works as God did from his. Let us therefore strive to enter that rest, so that no one may fall by the same sort of disobedience."

The New Testament books were written with design and purpose from one person to a group of others, but we can also prophetically use these concepts for our own lives. What God speaks to us today will be confirmed in scripture.

We are to cease from striving works that would make us feel as if we are attaining brownie points from heaven, but instead we should be striving to enter into his rest and live from that place.

If you cannot grasp any other concept in this book, focus on this one. Strive to enter his rest and start to live and move from that victorious place so that amazing fruit will manifest in your life.

Many things in our Christian walk are optional, such as if we decide to really pursue what God has put on our hearts. While it's completely up to us to decide if we want to embark on that journey, the basic evidence of faith is rest. Rest in your identity and rest in his promises!

Activation: What are some situations you are currently dealing with that you could put on the cross so that you can enter into his rest?

_____

_____

_____

_____

_____

_____

_____

_____

_____

_____

Let's Get Shift Done!   Millie 'Joy' Radosti

_____

_____

_____

_____

_____

Conclusion

There is power in our words, in our viewpoints, in how we train our eyes, hearts, and minds to look at our surroundings and determine the reality of the dreams and destiny that God's put in our hearts. We can either see the potential and call forth the testimony over a situation, or we can murder our purpose with our own mouth!

Matthew 5 talks about how if you so much as think of someone the wrong way—with anger or with lust—you have actually already committed murder and adultery.

Could you imagine if we believed that our thoughts and words (that lead to our actions) was actually had this kind of power? How might we live that out?

I'm a realistic person. I believe we need to call things forth as though they are without ignoring the reality of what is. In John 5, Jesus firsts asks the invalid man if he wants to be healed. "Do you want to be well?"

He didn't ignore the man's condition. But he saw the man with the eyes of faith. Jesus saw the situation and told the man to get up and walk.

Jesus was the most practical and prophetic person to ever walk the earth. He fully assessed the situation yet operated in 100 percent mountain-moving faith at the same time!

Let's read that passage to see exactly how Jesus accomplished this.

"Some time later, Jesus went up to Jerusalem for one of the Jewish festivals. Now there is in Jerusalem near the Sheep Gate a pool, which in Aramaic is called Bethesda and which is surrounded by five covered colonnades. Here a great number of disabled people used to lie—the blind, the lame, the paralyzed. One who was there had been an invalid for thirty-eight years. When Jesus saw him lying there and learned that he had been in this condition for a long time,

he asked him, "Do you want to get well?"
(John 5:1–6 NIV).

This question—"Do you want to get well?"—was his invitation to believe! Jesus was asking the man, "Do you *want* this?" With all the power and authority Jesus carried, do you think he needed to ask the man? Jesus wanted to know that this man really wanted to get well before he even made another move.

Verse seven says, "Sir," the invalid replied, "I have no one to help me into the pool when the water is stirred. While I am trying to get in, someone else goes down ahead of me."

This man is completely stuck in a victim mentality. "I have no one to help me. People cut in front of me. I can't receive my healing. My circumstances this, and my circumstances that. Yada, yada, yada." Let me ask you, if you had an issue that debilitated you for thirty-eight years and you were steps away from a pool where you knew you would receive your healing, what would stop you from getting in that pool? I know for me, absolutely *nothing* would stop me! I would somehow find a way to make it to the pool! But this man just had every excuse in the book.

"Then Jesus said to him, 'Get up! Pick up your mat and walk.' At once the man was cured; he picked up his mat and walked" (verse eight).

Before Jesus pulls the man out of his physical illness, he first pulls him out of his mental mindset. Notice he doesn't entertain the victim mentality that the man is hiding behind. He doesn't validate the man's excuses or dismiss the circumstance. He calls the man to rise above all of it and declares healing over his life. The man is not only set free from a physical illness, which is what most focus on when they read this passage. The man is set free from his own excuses. From his own defeated mindset. He now takes off from zero miles per hour to one hundred miles per hour—full throttle into a completely healthy and whole person, not only physically but mentally too.

Conclusion

Verse ten goes on to tell us, "The day on which this took place was a Sabbath, and so the Jewish leaders said to the man who had been healed, 'It is the Sabbath; the law forbids you to carry your mat.'"

When Jesus calls you out of your circumstances, sometimes he breaks all the rules. Sometimes rising up in your destiny crosses boundaries of culture and etiquette. Walking out your destiny might not always look like what we think it will look. Manifesting destiny doesn't happen through our man-made laws or boundaries.

But as you embark on this adventure and as you unwrap your future with God, you come to the place of ownership of what you have been given. No one can do this for you. You are the only person who can accomplish what God has set out for you to do!

You might have dreams in your life that are buried under some fear. It might not be buried miles deep, maybe just a couple layers of "life got in the way" or "I was scared to fail". Maybe some layers of "I entered season after season of putting others before myself". Or maybe it is even buried miles under guilt, fear, condemnation and shame of some unfortunate life paths you've been journeying.

Maybe you are already on the road to seeing your dreams manifest, but it's taken a lot of rabbit trails from what you originally expected. Maybe you've seen a lot of success but don't want to burn out and even thought you'd have progressed further by now.

This book is for you!

I want to take the dreams and passions buried under all those layers and see you manifest victoriously in success while thriving in your personal life. I've shared keys to motivation and focus, while developing your character and improving your overall quality of life by diving into key elements of your spiritual life. I know you've enjoyed not only gaining this practical knowledge but seeing the fruit of

Conclusion

practicing it in your lifestyle. Read this book again and again. Don't settle until you are reaching potential you are fully satisfied with!

Millie 'Joy' Radosti is a passionate author, pastor, teacher and church planter who longs to see see each individual discover their full potential and identity in Christ. Millie has also developed a unique coaching approach which she calls "Freedom Coaching." If you would like more information and/or are interested in coaching with Millie, please send an inquiry to Info@Church14.com.

Other Titles by Millie:

"Daddy Issues a New Life"
by Millie 'Joy' Radosti

Left to navigate the aftermath of an abusive home, she finds herself alone with no motivation to survive. Millie's story documents her road through abuse, self injury and numerous mental institution visits, among other challenges. After an unexpected twist gives Millie a new lease on life, she becomes empowered to impart hope and identity to a hurting and fatherless generation. Her journey from ashes to beauty is unlike any you've ever heard - a story of how our Heavenly Daddy Issues a New Life! CHURCH14.COM

189

Made in United States
Orlando, FL
14 July 2023

35051276R00108